PART I: UNDERSTANDING INTROVERSION — 3

Chapter 1: Introversion vs. Extroversion — 3
Chapter 2: The Science Behind — 6
Chapter 3: The Strengths of Introverts: Recognizing Your Unique Abilities — 10

PART II: THRIVING IN AN EXTROVERTED WORLD — 15

Chapter 4: Navigating Social Situations: Strategies for Introverts — 15
Chapter 5: Building Strong Relationships: Fostering Meaningful Connections — 20
Chapter 6: The Power of Networking: Tips for Introverted Professionals — 25

PART III: HARNESSING YOUR INTROVERTED POWER — 29

Chapter 7: Unleashing Your Creativity: Introverts as Innovators — 29
Chapter 8: Developing Leadership Skills: How Introverts Can Excel as Leaders — 33
Chapter 9: The Art of Public Speaking and Presentation for Introverts — 37

PART IV: PERSONAL GROWTH AND SELF-CARE — 41

Chapter 10: Setting Boundaries: Protecting Your Energy and Well-Being — 41
Chapter 11: Practicing Mindfulness and Meditation: A Path to Inner Peace — 46
Chapter 12: Building Confidence and Overcoming Self-Doubt — 51

PART V: CREATING AN INTROVERT-FRIENDLY ENVIRONMENT — 56

Chapter 13: Designing Your Personal Sanctuary: Creating Spaces that Nurture Your Soul — 56
Chapter 14: The Future of Introversion: Embracing a New Social Paradigm — 61

Conclusion: Your Introverted Journey - Embracing Your True Self and Thriving on Your Own Terms A concise summary of the key takeaways and actionable steps from each chapter Reinforcing the main points and providing a valuable reference for readers 64

Appendix: Resources for Introverts Recommended Books Podcasts and Videos Online Communities and Support Groups Networking Opportunities for Introverts Additional tools and resources to continue the self-improvement journey 65

Part I: Understanding Introversion

Chapter 1: Introversion vs. Extroversion: Debunking the Myths

Definitions of introversion and extroversion
In order to better understand introversion and extroversion, it is crucial to define these terms and explore their origins. Introversion and extroversion are personality traits that describe how individuals derive and expend their energy, as well as their preferences for social interaction and stimulation.
Introversion: Introverts are individuals who generally prefer quieter, more solitary environments and activities. They often derive their energy from spending time alone, engaging in introspective and reflective activities. Introverts typically prefer deep, meaningful conversations over small talk and may feel drained after prolonged social interactions.
Extroversion: Extroverts, on the other hand, are individuals who thrive in social settings and gain energy from interacting with others. They often seek out stimulating environments and activities, enjoying the company of others and engaging in lively conversations. Extroverts are typically more comfortable with small talk and may feel recharged after socializing.
It is essential to note that introversion and extroversion exist on a spectrum, and individuals may fall anywhere along this continuum. Some people may exhibit traits of both introversion and extroversion, often referred to as ambiverts. Furthermore, these traits are not fixed and may change over time or vary depending on the context and circumstances.
Understanding these definitions provides a solid foundation for exploring the nuances of introversion and extroversion, debunking common myths, and learning how to thrive as an introvert in an extroverted world.

Common misconceptions about introverts and extroverts
Despite increasing awareness about introversion and extroversion, several misconceptions continue to persist. These misconceptions can lead to misunderstandings and create barriers in personal and professional relationships. Here, we will address some of the most common misconceptions about introverts and extroverts.

Misconception 1: Introverts are shy, and extroverts are outgoing
While it's true that some introverts may be shy, it is not an inherent characteristic of introversion. Introversion is more about where an individual derives their energy, whereas shyness is a feeling of anxiety or discomfort in social situations. An extrovert can also be shy, despite their preference for social interaction.

Misconception 2: Introverts don't like people, and extroverts don't enjoy solitude
Introverts can enjoy spending time with others and building meaningful relationships, but they often prefer smaller, more intimate gatherings and may require time alone to recharge. Similarly, extroverts can appreciate moments of solitude and quiet reflection, even though they generally derive energy from social interactions.

Misconception 3: Introverts are always quiet, and extroverts are always talkative
While introverts might be more inclined to listen and observe before speaking, they can be quite talkative and expressive when discussing topics they are passionate about. Conversely, extroverts may not always dominate conversations and can be excellent listeners when engaged in meaningful discussions.

Misconception 4: Introverts are not good leaders, and extroverts are natural leaders
Introverts can be highly effective leaders, bringing qualities such as empathy, deep thinking, and strong listening skills to their leadership roles. Extroverts may have a more visible leadership style, but introverted leaders can be just as successful in guiding and motivating their teams.

Misconception 5: Introversion and extroversion are fixed traits
As mentioned earlier, introversion and extroversion exist on a spectrum, and an individual's preferences can change over time or depending on the context. It is essential to recognize that people are complex and multifaceted, and their personalities cannot be defined solely by their introverted or extroverted tendencies.

By debunking these common misconceptions, we can foster greater understanding and acceptance of introverts and extroverts, paving the way for more harmonious relationships and collaboration in various aspects of life.

The Introversion-Extroversion Spectrum

The introversion-extroversion spectrum is a continuum that represents the range of preferences and tendencies related to social interaction, energy, and stimulation. Rather than categorizing individuals as purely introverted or extroverted, the spectrum acknowledges that people can exhibit traits from both ends of the continuum and that these traits can vary depending on the situation or over time.

Here are some key aspects of the introversion-extroversion spectrum:

1. **Ambiverts**: Many people fall somewhere in the middle of the introversion-extroversion spectrum, displaying traits from both introversion and extroversion. These individuals are known as ambiverts. Ambiverts can adapt their behaviour based on the context or their mood, sometimes preferring solitude and introspection, and at other times seeking social interactions and stimulation.
2. **Situational factors**: An individual's position on the introversion-extroversion spectrum can be influenced by situational factors, such as the environment, the people present, or their level of familiarity with a particular setting. For example, an introvert might feel more extroverted among close friends or when discussing a topic they are passionate about, while an extrovert might lean towards introversion in an unfamiliar or uncomfortable setting.
3. **Fluidity over time**: An individual's preferences for introversion or extroversion can change over time as they grow and develop. Life experiences, personal growth, and changing circumstances can all contribute to shifts in one's position on the introversion-extroversion spectrum. For example, a person who was predominantly extroverted during their college years might find themselves becoming more introverted as they age and their priorities shift.
4. **Understanding and acceptance**: Recognizing the introversion-extroversion spectrum helps to promote understanding and acceptance of individual differences. By acknowledging that people can exhibit a range of introverted and extroverted traits, we can foster greater empathy and appreciation for the unique qualities that each person brings to their relationships, workplaces, and social settings.
5.

In summary, the introversion-extroversion spectrum highlights the complexity and diversity of human personality traits. By embracing the idea that individuals can exhibit varying degrees of introversion and extroversion, we can work towards a more inclusive and empathetic understanding of the people around us.

Chapter 2: The Science Behind Introversion: How Your Brain Works

The Role of Neurotransmitters in Introversion
Neurotransmitters are essential chemicals that transmit signals between nerve cells or neurons, facilitating communication within the brain and throughout the body. Research has revealed that the levels and activity of certain neurotransmitters play a significant role in introversion and extroversion, influencing individuals' preferences for social interaction, stimulation, and other behaviours.
Two primary neurotransmitters involved in introversion are dopamine and acetylcholine:
1. **Dopamine**: Dopamine is a neurotransmitter associated with reward, motivation, and pleasure-seeking behaviours. It plays a critical role in the brain's reward system, which influences an individual's response to external stimuli and their propensity to seek out new and exciting experiences. Extroverts tend to have a more active dopamine system, making them more responsive to social and environmental stimuli. As a result, extroverts often seek out situations that provide novelty, excitement, and social interaction.

In contrast, introverts are less sensitive to the effects of dopamine, displaying a more muted response to external stimuli. This reduced sensitivity results in introverts being less motivated by the same level of stimulation that excites extroverts. Instead, introverts often prefer quieter, more solitary environments that allow for reflection and introspection.

2. **Acetylcholine**: Acetylcholine is another neurotransmitter that plays a vital role in introversion. It is involved in various functions, including learning, memory, and the ability to focus and maintain attention. Acetylcholine is more dominant in introverts, contributing to their preference for activities that involve deep thought, concentration, and introspection. When engaging in these activities, introverts experience a sense of reward and satisfaction, like the dopamine-driven rewards that extroverts receive from social interactions and external stimuli.

In summary, the balance and activity of neurotransmitters such as dopamine and acetylcholine play a crucial role in shaping introverted and extroverted tendencies. By understanding the underlying neurochemistry of introversion, we can appreciate the unique preferences, strengths, and motivations of introverts and better support their personal and professional growth.

How Introvert and Extrovert Brains Process Information Differently

The differences between introvert and extrovert brains extend beyond neurotransmitter activity. Research has shown that the ways in which introvert and extrovert brains process information also vary, leading to distinct preferences, behaviours, and cognitive strengths.

Here are some key differences in how introvert and extrovert brains process information:

1. **Cerebral blood flow and neural pathways**: Studies have shown that introvert and extrovert brains have distinct patterns of cerebral blood flow, suggesting that they utilize different neural pathways when processing information. Introvert brains tend to have more blood flow in regions associated with internal experiences, such as introspection, memory, and problem-solving. This increased activity in internal-processing regions contributes to introverts' preference for deep thought and reflection.

In contrast, extrovert brains show more blood flow in areas associated with sensory processing and external stimuli, indicating that they are more attuned to their surroundings and social interactions.

2. **Prefrontal cortex activity**: The prefrontal cortex, a region of the brain responsible for executive functions such as decision-making, planning, and impulse control, has been found to be more active in introverts than extroverts. This heightened activity may contribute to introverts' cautious and reflective approach to decision-making, as well as their ability to focus on complex tasks for extended periods.

3. **Response to novelty**: Research has shown that introverts and extroverts differ in their brain's response to novel stimuli. Extroverts tend to display a more pronounced response to new experiences, people, and environments, as evidenced by increased activity in their brain's reward system. This heightened response to novelty drives extroverts to seek out new experiences and engage in social interactions more readily than introverts.

On the other hand, introverts may require more time to process and adapt to new situations, often preferring familiar and predictable environments that allow for introspection and contemplation.

4. **Processing speed and depth**: Introverts are often characterized by a more deliberate and in-depth processing style, whereas extroverts tend to process information more quickly and superficially. This difference in processing speed and depth can manifest in various aspects of cognition, such as problem-solving, decision-making, and learning.

In summary, the differences in how introvert and extrovert brains process information contribute to their unique cognitive strengths, preferences, and behaviours. By understanding and appreciating these distinctions, we can foster greater empathy and support for both introverts and extroverts in our personal and professional relationships.

The Impact of Stimulation on Introverts and Extroverts
The level of stimulation in each environment or situation has a significant impact on the comfort, performance, and well-being of both introverts and extroverts. Each group responds differently to varying degrees of stimulation, which in turn influences their preferences for social interaction, work settings, and leisure activities.

Here are some ways in which introverts and extroverts are affected by stimulation:

1. **Introverts and stimulation**: Introverts tend to have a lower threshold for stimulation, which means that they can become overwhelmed or overstimulated more quickly than extroverts. In highly stimulating environments or situations, such as crowded parties or noisy workplaces, introverts may experience increased stress, anxiety, or mental fatigue. This sensitivity to stimulation leads introverts to seek out quieter, more tranquil settings that allow for reflection and introspection.

To cope with overstimulation, introverts often need periods of solitude and downtime to recharge their mental and emotional energy. They may also benefit from engaging in calming activities, such as reading, journaling, or spending time in nature.

2. **Extroverts and stimulation**: Extroverts, on the other hand, have a higher threshold for stimulation and often thrive in environments that provide ample sensory input, social interaction, and novelty. The extrovert brain's heightened response to external stimuli makes them more drawn to lively and engaging situations, where they can socialize and actively participate in their surroundings.

Extroverts are more likely to feel energized and invigorated by stimulating environments, making them well-suited for careers and hobbies that involve socializing, teamwork, and dynamic settings. However, it is essential for extroverts to recognize their need for balance and ensure that they also allocate time for reflection, self-care, and relaxation.

In summary, the impact of stimulation on introverts and extroverts is a crucial factor in shaping their preferences, behaviours, and well-being. By understanding and respecting these differences, we can create more inclusive environments and better support the unique needs of both introverts and extroverts in our personal and professional lives.

Relevant Research and Expert Opinions
Numerous studies and experts have contributed to our understanding of introversion and extroversion. Here are some key findings and expert opinions that provide valuable insights into the science, strengths, and challenges of introversion:

1. **Carl Jung's Theory of Psychological Types**: The Swiss psychiatrist Carl Jung introduced the concept of introversion and extroversion in his theory of psychological types, laying the foundation for our modern understanding of these traits. Jung posited that introverts are more focused on their inner world of thoughts and feelings, while extroverts are oriented toward the external world of people and experiences.
2. **The research of Hans Eysenck**: Psychologist Hans Eysenck built upon Jung's work, developing a biological model of introversion and extroversion. Eysenck suggested that these traits are linked to differences in the brain's arousal systems, with introverts having higher baseline levels of arousal and extroverts having lower baseline arousal. As a result, introverts seek out lower levels of stimulation to maintain optimal arousal, while extroverts require more stimulation to reach the same optimal state.
3. **Jerome Kagan's research on temperament**: Developmental psychologist Jerome Kagan conducted ground-breaking research on temperament, revealing that some individuals are born with a predisposition toward introversion or extroversion. Kagan's studies on infants and children found that "high-reactive" infants, who showed heightened sensitivity to stimuli, were more likely to develop introverted personalities, while "low-reactive" infants were more likely to become extroverted.
4. **Susan Cain's work on introversion**: Susan Cain, author of the best-selling book "Quiet: The Power of Introverts in a World That Can't Stop Talking," has become a leading advocate for introverts. Cain highlights the unique strengths and contributions of introverts in various domains, such as leadership, creativity, and problem-solving. She emphasizes the importance of valuing and embracing introversion in a society that often prioritizes extroverted traits.
5. **Elaine Aron's research on Highly Sensitive Persons (HSPs)**: Psychologist Elaine Aron has contributed to our understanding of sensitivity and its relationship to introversion through her work on Highly Sensitive Persons (HSPs). Aron posits that around 15-20% of the population has a highly sensitive temperament, characterized by increased responsiveness to physical, emotional, and social stimuli. While not all HSPs are introverts, there is a significant overlap between the two traits, highlighting the importance of understanding and accommodating sensitivity in various settings.

These studies and expert opinions have advanced our understanding of introversion and its implications for personal and professional life. By staying informed about the latest research, we can continue to support and empower introverts in our communities and help them thrive in an extroverted world.

Chapter 3: The Strengths of Introverts:
Recognizing Your Unique Qualities

Deep Thinking and Reflection
One of the most notable strengths of introverts is their capacity for deep thinking and reflection. Due to their preference for solitary activities and their sensitivity to external stimuli, introverts often spend more time engaged in introspection, considering various aspects of their thoughts, feelings, and experiences. This inclination toward deep thought allows introverts to develop a rich inner life, which can contribute to their personal growth, creativity, and problem-solving abilities.
Here are some ways in which introverts' deep thinking and reflection can be advantageous:
1. **Self-awareness**: Introverts' tendency to engage in introspection can lead to a heightened sense of self-awareness. By spending time examining their thoughts, emotions, and motivations, introverts can develop a better understanding of themselves, their values, and their personal goals. This self-awareness can help introverts make informed decisions and maintain a strong sense of authenticity in their personal and professional lives.
2. **Critical thinking**: Introverts often excel at critical thinking, a skill that involves analysing, evaluating, and synthesizing information to form well-reasoned judgments and conclusions. Their preference for deep thought and reflection allows introverts to consider multiple perspectives and assess complex ideas or situations more thoroughly than their extroverted counterparts.
3. **Problem-solving**: Introverts' propensity for deep thinking can also be an asset in problem-solving situations. Their ability to analyse problems from various angles, consider potential outcomes, and weigh the pros and cons of different solutions makes them effective problem solvers. Introverts are often able to approach challenges with a calm and measured demeanour, leading to well-thought-out decisions and innovative solutions.
4. **Creativity**: Many introverts possess a rich imagination and a strong creative streak, thanks to their deep thinking and reflective nature. Introverts often draw inspiration from their inner world, using their thoughts, feelings, and experiences as a springboard for creative expression. This creativity can manifest in various ways, such as writing, art, music, or innovative thinking in professional contexts.

5. **Mindfulness**: Introverts' inclination toward reflection and introspection can also foster a greater sense of mindfulness. By being more attuned to their thoughts and emotions, introverts can develop a deeper connection with themselves and their surroundings, leading to increased emotional intelligence, empathy, and resilience.

By recognizing and embracing these strengths, introverts can harness their unique qualities to excel in various aspects of their lives. Whether it's navigating personal relationships, pursuing creative endeavours, or solving complex problems, introverts' deep thinking and reflective nature can be a powerful asset.

Empathy and Listening Skills

Another significant strength of introverts is their innate capacity for empathy and active listening. Empathy is the ability to understand and share the feelings of others, while active listening involves fully concentrating, understanding, and responding to what someone else is saying. These qualities allow introverts to forge strong connections with others and offer valuable support and insights in personal and professional contexts.

Here are some aspects of introverts' empathy and listening skills that make them stand out:

1. **Attentiveness**: Introverts are often highly attentive to the emotions, needs, and concerns of those around them. Their sensitivity and introspective nature make them more tuned into subtle cues, such as body language, tone of voice, and facial expressions, allowing them to better understand others' feelings and perspectives.
2. **Active listening**: Introverts excel at active listening, a skill that involves fully focusing on the speaker, absorbing their message, and responding thoughtfully. Introverts' preference for one-on-one conversations and their natural ability to concentrate on the speaker make them effective listeners who can provide valuable feedback and insights.
3. **Emotional intelligence**: Introverts' empathy and listening skills contribute to their high emotional intelligence (EQ). Emotional intelligence refers to the ability to recognize, understand, and manage one's emotions and those of others. Introverts' heightened self-awareness and sensitivity to others' emotions enable them to navigate social situations with empathy and understanding, even if they may sometimes find these situations challenging.
4. **Building trust**: Introverts' empathetic nature and willingness to listen can help build trust in relationships. By taking the time to understand others' perspectives and offering genuine support, introverts can foster a sense of connection and trust with friends, family members, and colleagues.

5. **Conflict resolution**: Introverts' empathy and listening skills can also be advantageous in conflict resolution. Their ability to understand different viewpoints and remain calm in tense situations allows them to mediate disputes effectively, facilitating open communication and fostering compromise.

By leveraging their empathy and listening skills, introverts can forge meaningful connections and make valuable contributions in both their personal and professional lives. By being present, understanding, and supportive, introverts can help others feel heard, respected, and valued, leading to more fulfilling and harmonious relationships.

Creativity and Problem-Solving Abilities
Introverts are often gifted with exceptional creativity and problem-solving abilities, stemming from their introspective nature and deep thinking. These qualities enable introverts to approach challenges with unique perspectives, find innovative solutions, and excel in various personal and professional contexts.

Here are some ways in which introverts' creativity and problem-solving abilities can be advantageous:
   1. **Innovative thinking**: Introverts' capacity for deep thought and reflection allows them to see beyond conventional wisdom and explore new ideas, concepts, or approaches. This innovative thinking can lead to ground-breaking discoveries, novel inventions, or fresh perspectives on existing problems or challenges.
   2. **Attention to detail**: Introverts are known for their keen attention to detail, which can be invaluable when solving complex problems or working on intricate projects. Their ability to focus and notice subtle nuances enables them to identify patterns, spot inconsistencies, or uncover hidden connections that others might overlook.
   3. **Persistence**: Introverts often display a strong sense of determination and persistence when working on tasks or projects that align with their passions and interests. This perseverance can be a significant asset in problem-solving, as it enables introverts to push through obstacles, refine their ideas, and ultimately find the best solution.
   4. **Adaptability**: Introverts' creativity and problem-solving abilities can also make them highly adaptable in various situations. Their willingness to explore different approaches, learn from mistakes, and embrace new ideas enables them to adjust and thrive in changing circumstances, both personally and professionally.
   5. **Collaboration**: Although introverts may prefer working independently, their creativity and problem-solving skills can be valuable assets in collaborative settings. Introverts' ability to listen and empathize with others, coupled with their unique perspectives, can contribute to a well-rounded team dynamic and lead to more innovative and effective solutions.

By embracing and nurturing their creativity and problem-solving abilities, introverts can leverage these strengths to excel in various personal and professional pursuits. Whether it's developing inventive solutions to pressing issues, contributing fresh ideas to collaborative projects, or exploring new creative outlets, introverts have much to offer in a world that increasingly values innovation and adaptability.

Real-Life Examples of Introverts Leveraging Their Strengths
Introverts have made significant contributions in various fields by harnessing their unique strengths. These real-life examples showcase how introverts can excel by leveraging their deep thinking, empathy, creativity, and problem-solving abilities:

1. **Albert Einstein**: The renowned physicist was known for his introverted nature and deep thinking. Einstein's ability to focus intensely on complex problems and consider multiple perspectives allowed him to develop the ground-breaking theory of relativity, which transformed our understanding of the universe.
2. **J.K. Rowling**: The author of the Harry Potter series, J.K. Rowling, is a self-proclaimed introvert who used her creativity and imagination to craft one of the most successful book series of all time. Rowling's preference for solitude and introspection enabled her to develop the intricate world of Hogwarts and its memorable characters.
3. **Rosa Parks**: Civil rights activist Rosa Parks, known for her quiet determination and introverted nature, played a pivotal role in the American Civil Rights Movement. Parks' strength and resolve in the face of adversity, coupled with her empathy for others, helped spark significant change in American society.
4. **Bill Gates**: The co-founder of Microsoft, Bill Gates, is an introvert who has used his deep thinking and problem-solving abilities to revolutionize the technology industry. Gates' ability to focus on complex issues and innovate has led to the creation of some of the most impactful technological advancements in modern history.
5. **Eleanor Roosevelt**: Former First Lady Eleanor Roosevelt was known for her introverted nature and her ability to listen empathetically to others. Her strong sense of empathy and dedication to helping others led her to become a champion for human rights and social justice, both during her time as First Lady and in her later years.
6. **Isaac Newton**: Sir Isaac Newton, one of the most influential scientists of all time, was a highly introverted individual. His ability to focus intensely on his work and think deeply about complex problems led to the development of the laws of motion and universal gravitation, which laid the groundwork for classical mechanics.

These inspiring examples demonstrate that introverts can achieve remarkable success and make a significant impact in various fields by harnessing their unique strengths. By embracing their introverted nature and leveraging their deep thinking, empathy, creativity, and problem-solving abilities, introverts can excel in their chosen pursuits and contribute meaningfully to the world.

Part II: Thriving in an Extroverted World

Chapter 4: Navigating Social Situations: Strategies for Introverts

Preparing for Social Events
While introverts may find social events challenging, they can develop strategies to make these situations more manageable and enjoyable. Proper preparation can help introverts feel more at ease and confident when attending social gatherings, allowing them to make the most of these experiences. Here are some tips for preparing for social events as an introvert:

1. **Know your limits**: Understand your energy levels and set boundaries for yourself. Determine how long you can comfortably engage in social activities before feeling drained and plan accordingly. This may mean attending an event for a limited time or ensuring you have a quiet space to retreat to if needed.
2. **Research the event**: Familiarize yourself with the event's purpose, location, and expected attendees. Knowing what to expect can help reduce anxiety and make you feel more prepared. If possible, connect with someone you know who will be attending the event, as this can provide a sense of familiarity and support.
3. **Set goals**: Establish specific, achievable goals for the event. These goals can be as simple as introducing yourself to a certain number of people, engaging in a few meaningful conversations, or exchanging contact information with potential networking contacts. Setting goals can help you feel more focused and purposeful during the event.
4. **Prepare conversation topics**: Think about topics of conversation that interest you or that you feel comfortable discussing. Having a few conversation starters in mind can help reduce anxiety about small talk and make it easier to engage with others. Additionally, consider asking open-ended questions to encourage others to share their thoughts and experiences, which can lead to more meaningful conversations.

5. **Practice self-care**: Ensure you're taking care of yourself physically, mentally, and emotionally before the event. This can include getting adequate rest, eating well, engaging in relaxation techniques, or setting aside time for activities that recharge you. Prioritizing self-care can help you feel more energized and ready to engage in social situations.
6. **Plan your exit strategy**: Knowing when and how you'll leave the event can provide a sense of control and reduce anxiety. Having a clear exit strategy can help you feel more at ease during the event, knowing that you have a plan in place if you need to leave.

By incorporating these strategies, introverts can prepare for social events in a way that aligns with their needs and preferences. With proper preparation, introverts can not only navigate social situations more comfortably but also leverage their unique strengths to make meaningful connections and enjoy the experience.

Managing Small Talk and Conversation

Small talk can be challenging for introverts, as they often prefer deeper, more meaningful conversations. However, mastering the art of small talk is essential for building connections and navigating social situations effectively. Here are some tips for managing small talk and conversation as an introvert:

1. **Embrace the power of listening**: Remember that you don't always have to be the one speaking. Introverts excel at active listening, which is an essential component of successful conversations. Show genuine interest in what the other person is saying and ask open-ended questions to encourage them to share more about themselves.
2. **Find common ground**: Look for topics of mutual interest to create a connection with the other person. This can be as simple as discussing a recent movie, a shared hobby, or an experience at the event. Building on common ground can help the conversation flow more smoothly and create a sense of rapport.
3. **Share personal anecdotes**: While introverts might be hesitant to share personal details, opening a little can make the conversation more engaging and help others connect with you. Share a relevant story or experience that relates to the topic at hand, but remember to balance your sharing with active listening to create a two-way conversation.
4. **Practice active listening**: When engaging in conversation, focus on what the other person is saying and respond thoughtfully. This can involve nodding, maintaining eye contact, and offering verbal affirmations. Active listening not only shows that you're interested in the conversation, but it also encourages the other person to open and share more.

5. **Be mindful of body language**: Nonverbal communication plays a significant role in how others perceive us. Maintain open and welcoming body language by making eye contact, smiling, and keeping your arms uncrossed. This can help create a more comfortable and inviting atmosphere for conversation.
6. **Learn to gracefully exit conversations**: Sometimes, small talk can lead to dead ends or awkward silences. In these cases, it's essential to know how to gracefully exit the conversation. You can do this by politely excusing yourself to get a drink, introducing the person to someone else, or mentioning that you need to catch up with another attendee. Having a few exit strategies in mind can help you feel more in control and at ease in social situations.

By implementing these tips, introverts can manage small talk and conversations more effectively, allowing them to navigate social situations with confidence. With practice and persistence, introverts can develop the skills necessary to build connections, foster relationships, and thrive in various social settings.

Dealing with Social Anxiety

Social anxiety can be a significant challenge for introverts, making it difficult to engage in social situations and form connections with others. However, it's important to remember that it's possible to manage social anxiety and develop coping strategies that allow you to feel more at ease in social settings. Here are some tips for dealing with social anxiety as an introvert:

1. **Acknowledge and accept your feelings**: Recognize that it's normal to feel anxious in social situations and that many people experience similar feelings. Accepting your anxiety, rather than trying to suppress it, can help you develop a more compassionate and understanding perspective towards yourself.
2. **Focus on your breath**: When feeling overwhelmed or anxious, take a moment to focus on your breath. Breathing deeply and slowly can help calm your nervous system and reduce anxiety. Practice mindfulness or meditation techniques to further enhance your ability to manage stress and anxiety.
3. **Challenge negative thoughts**: Social anxiety often stems from negative thoughts and beliefs about oneself. Identify these thoughts and challenge their accuracy. Replace them with more realistic and positive affirmations, which can help to shift your mindset and reduce anxiety.
4. **Start small**: Gradually expose yourself to social situations, starting with less intimidating environments and working your way up to more challenging ones. This can help you build confidence and develop coping strategies that will serve you well in a variety of social settings.

5. **Set realistic expectations**: Understand that it's okay not to be the life of the party or to have perfect social interactions. Setting realistic expectations for yourself can help reduce the pressure you feel in social situations, making it easier to manage anxiety.
6. **Develop a support system**: Surround yourself with supportive friends or family members who understand your introverted nature and social anxiety. Having a support system can provide encouragement, understanding, and guidance as you navigate social situations.
7. **Seek professional help**: If social anxiety is significantly impacting your life and well-being, consider seeking the help of a mental health professional. Therapy, such as cognitive-behavioural therapy (CBT), can be beneficial in addressing and managing social anxiety.

By incorporating these strategies, introverts can learn to manage their social anxiety more effectively, allowing them to participate in social situations with greater confidence and ease. Over time, practicing these techniques can help introverts develop resilience and adaptability in the face of social challenges, ultimately enabling them to thrive in an extroverted world.

Specific Actions, Techniques, or Exercises for Improving Social Skills

Developing strong social skills is essential for introverts to navigate social situations and build meaningful connections. Here are some specific actions, techniques, or exercises that can help improve social skills:

1. **Role-playing**: Practice social scenarios with a trusted friend or family member. This can help you become more comfortable with different situations and develop your conversational skills in a low-pressure environment.
2. **Active listening exercises**: Improve your listening skills by practicing active listening with others. Focus on what the other person is saying, and try to avoid interrupting or thinking about your response while they're speaking. After they finish, summarize what they said to ensure you fully understood their message.
3. **Observation**: Pay attention to how others navigate social situations, particularly those who seem to have strong social skills. Observe their body language, tone of voice, and conversational techniques, and consider how you might incorporate similar strategies into your own social interactions.
4. **Join social clubs or groups**: Participate in clubs or groups focused on your interests, where you can meet like-minded individuals. This can provide a supportive environment for practicing social skills and building connections.

5. **Develop an elevator pitch**: Prepare a brief introduction of yourself, including your name, occupation, and a few personal interests. This can serve as an effective icebreaker in social situations and help you feel more confident when meeting new people.
6. **Practice storytelling**: Develop your storytelling abilities by sharing personal anecdotes or experiences with others. This can help you engage in more meaningful conversations and become a more captivating conversationalist.
7. **Assertiveness training**: Learn how to express your thoughts, feelings, and needs in a clear and respectful manner. This can help you build stronger relationships and improve your ability to navigate social situations effectively.
8. **Body language awareness**: Be mindful of your nonverbal communication, such as eye contact, facial expressions, and posture. Practicing open and confident body language can make a significant difference in how others perceive you and your level of comfort in social situations.
9. **Ask for feedback**: Request constructive feedback from friends or family members about your social skills. This can help you identify areas for improvement and gain valuable insights into how others perceive you.
10. **Set social goals**: Establish specific, achievable social goals, such as attending a certain number of events, engaging in conversations with new people, or deepening existing relationships. Tracking your progress towards these goals can help you stay motivated and focused on your social skill development.

By consistently practicing these actions, techniques, and exercises, introverts can develop and improve their social skills, making it easier to navigate and thrive in various social settings. Over time, these efforts can lead to increased confidence, stronger connections, and a more fulfilling social life.

Chapter 5: Building Strong Relationships: Fostering Meaningful Connections

Introverts and Friendship
Introverts often have a unique approach to friendship, prioritizing quality over quantity and seeking deeper, more meaningful connections with others. While introverts may have fewer friends compared to their extroverted counterparts, the relationships they form tend to be strong and long-lasting. Understanding the introvert's perspective on friendship can help introverts foster meaningful connections and cultivate fulfilling friendships. In this section, we will discuss:

1. **The value of deep connections**: Introverts often prefer having a few close friends with whom they can share their thoughts, feelings, and experiences. These deep connections provide a sense of belonging, emotional support, and mutual understanding that introverts greatly value in their friendships.
2. **One-on-one interactions**: Introverts tend to feel most comfortable and connected in one-on-one settings, where they can engage in deeper conversations and truly get to know the other person. Scheduling regular one-on-one time with friends can help introverts maintain and strengthen their friendships.
3. **Quality over quantity**: Embrace the fact that having a smaller circle of friends can be just as fulfilling as having numerous acquaintances. Introverts should focus on nurturing their existing friendships and developing strong connections with a select group of individuals, rather than trying to keep up with an extensive social network.
4. **Shared interests and activities**: Building friendships around shared interests and activities can create a natural foundation for meaningful connections. Joining clubs, groups, or classes focused on your passions can provide an opportunity to meet like-minded individuals and form lasting friendships.
5. **Maintaining boundaries**: Introverts need time alone to recharge and reflect, so it's essential to establish and communicate personal boundaries within friendships. Be open with your friends about your need for solitude and alone time, and work together to find a balance that meets both parties' needs.
6. **Developing emotional intelligence**: Developing emotional intelligence can help introverts better understand and empathize with their friends' feelings, needs, and perspectives. Practicing active listening, empathy, and effective communication can help introverts build stronger, more fulfilling friendships.

7. **Cultivating trust and vulnerability**: Trust and vulnerability are essential components of deep, meaningful friendships. Introverts should strive to create a safe space within their friendships where both parties feel comfortable sharing their thoughts, feelings, and experiences openly and honestly.

By understanding and embracing their unique approach to friendship, introverts can foster meaningful connections that provide emotional support, companionship, and a sense of belonging. Cultivating strong friendships can significantly contribute to an introvert's overall well-being and personal growth, allowing them to thrive in their relationships and in life.

Developing Romantic Relationships

For introverts, developing romantic relationships can be both rewarding and challenging. Their preference for deep connections and one-on-one interactions can lead to strong, intimate partnerships, but they may also face unique hurdles in finding and maintaining these relationships. Here are some strategies for introverts to successfully navigate the world of dating and romantic relationships:

1. **Embrace your introverted qualities**: Recognize that your introverted traits, such as thoughtfulness, empathy, and the ability to listen deeply, are assets in romantic relationships. Embrace these qualities and showcase them authentically in your interactions with potential partners.
2. **Be open and honest about your needs**: Communicate your introverted nature and the need for alone time to your potential partner early in the relationship. Establishing open communication about your needs can help ensure both you and your partner understand and respect each other's boundaries and preferences.
3. **Choose the right dating platforms**: Consider using dating platforms that cater to your preferences and comfort level. For example, introverts may find more success on dating apps that emphasize compatibility and shared interests, rather than those that focus on superficial connections and high-energy social interactions.
4. **Engage in shared activities**: Participate in activities that align with your interests and allow for meaningful connection. This could include joining clubs, attending workshops, or volunteering for events where you are likely to meet people with similar values and interests.
5. **Take your time**: Introverts often prefer to build connections slowly, allowing trust and intimacy to develop gradually. Give yourself and your potential partner the time and space needed to truly get to know each other, without feeling pressured to rush the process.

6. **Develop effective communication skills**: Good communication is crucial in any relationship. Practice active listening, empathy, and assertiveness to ensure you and your partner can openly discuss your thoughts, feelings, and needs.
7. **Manage conflict constructively**: Disagreements are a natural part of any relationship. Learn to manage conflict in a constructive manner by focusing on understanding your partner's perspective, maintaining open communication, and seeking mutually satisfying solutions.
8. **Maintain a balance between personal and shared space**: In any romantic relationship, it's important to strike a balance between spending time together and allowing for personal space. Work with your partner to establish a routine that meets both of your needs for connection and solitude.

By adopting these strategies, introverts can navigate the complexities of romantic relationships more effectively, ultimately fostering strong, lasting connections that enrich their lives. Embracing their unique qualities and developing effective communication skills can help introverts create fulfilling and supportive partnerships based on mutual understanding and respect.

Maintaining Long-Lasting Connections

For introverts, maintaining long-lasting connections requires a delicate balance between nurturing their relationships and preserving their own need for solitude and reflection. By focusing on open communication, mutual understanding, and shared experiences, introverts can cultivate strong, enduring connections with friends, romantic partners, and family members. Here are some strategies for maintaining long-lasting connections:

1. **Prioritize regular communication**: Try to maintain consistent communication with the people you care about, even if it's just a simple text message, email, or phone call. Consistent check-ins show that you value the relationship and are invested in maintaining the connection.
2. **Schedule quality time together**: Plan regular one-on-one time with your loved ones, focusing on activities that allow for deep conversation and connection. Make these occasions a priority and honour your commitments to demonstrate your dedication to the relationship.
3. **Be present and engaged**: When spending time with others, make a conscious effort to be present and engaged in the conversation. Active listening and genuine interest in their thoughts, feelings, and experiences can go a long way in nurturing long-lasting connections.

4. **Celebrate important milestones**: Acknowledge and celebrate the significant events and milestones in your loved ones' lives, such as birthdays, anniversaries, promotions, and achievements. These gestures show that you care and are invested in their happiness and well-being.
5. **Offer support and encouragement**: Be a reliable source of support and encouragement for your loved ones, offering a listening ear, helpful advice, or a shoulder to lean on when needed. Cultivating a supportive environment within your relationships will strengthen your bonds and create a sense of trust and security.
6. **Develop shared interests and experiences**: Invest in shared experiences and interests with your loved ones, creating lasting memories and deepening your connection. This can include traveling together, joining a club or group, or simply exploring new hobbies and activities as a team.
7. **Practice empathy and understanding**: Strive to understand and empathize with your loved ones' perspectives, even if they differ from your own. Demonstrating compassion and understanding can help create an atmosphere of mutual respect and acceptance, fostering stronger connections.
8. **Grow and evolve together**: Relationships are dynamic, and change is inevitable. Embrace the changes and growth that occur over time, and be open to adapting your relationship to meet the evolving needs of both parties. This flexibility and willingness to grow can contribute significantly to the longevity of your connections.

By implementing these strategies, introverts can maintain long-lasting connections that enrich their lives and provide a strong support network. With intention, effort, and open communication, introverts can cultivate deep, enduring relationships that withstand the test of time.

Case Studies and Expert Advice

To provide a deeper understanding of how introverts can foster meaningful connections, we will explore case studies and expert advice that demonstrate the principles discussed in this chapter. These examples offer insights and guidance to help introverts navigate the complexities of building and maintaining strong relationships.

Case Study 1: The Introverted Listener

Jane is an introvert who has always valued her ability to listen deeply and empathize with others. As a result, she has developed a close-knit group of friends who appreciate her understanding nature. Jane's friendships are built on trust and mutual support, with each person feeling heard and valued.

Expert Advice: Dr. Laurie Helgoe, author of "Introvert Power: Why Your Inner Life Is Your Hidden Strength," suggests that introverts' listening skills and empathy are valuable assets in building strong connections. By genuinely engaging with others and providing a safe space for open communication, introverts can foster meaningful relationships that are built on trust and understanding.

Case Study 2: Shared Interests
Michael is an introverted artist who struggled to find like-minded individuals with whom he could connect. By joining a local art collective, he discovered a group of people who shared his passion for creativity. Over time, Michael formed close friendships with several members of the group, with their shared interests providing a foundation for deep, meaningful connections.

Expert Advice: Susan Cain, author of "Quiet: The Power of Introverts in a World That Can't Stop Talking," emphasizes the importance of finding and engaging with people who share your interests and values. For introverts, connecting with others through shared activities and interests can be a powerful means of fostering lasting relationships.

Case Study 3: Communicating Boundaries in Romantic Relationships
Emma, an introvert, found herself in a romantic relationship with an extrovert who enjoyed frequent social gatherings. Initially, Emma struggled to balance her need for solitude with her partner's desire for socialization. By openly discussing her introverted nature and establishing boundaries, Emma and her partner were able to find a balance that met both of their needs.

Expert Advice: Dr. Marti Olsen Laney, author of "The Introvert Advantage: How Quiet People Can Thrive in an Extrovert World," recommends that introverts communicate their needs and boundaries early in a relationship. By establishing open communication and mutual understanding, introverts can create strong, lasting partnerships that respect and honour everyone's unique qualities.

These case studies and expert advice demonstrate the potential for introverts to foster meaningful connections in various aspects of their lives. By embracing their unique qualities, seeking out shared interests, and communicating their needs and boundaries, introverts can cultivate strong, enduring relationships that provide emotional support, companionship, and a sense of belonging.

Chapter 6: The Power of Networking: Tips for Introverted Professionals

Overcoming Networking Challenges
For introverts, networking can often feel overwhelming and intimidating, as it typically involves engaging with strangers and navigating group dynamics. However, with the right strategies and mindset, introverts can overcome these challenges and leverage their unique qualities to build valuable professional connections. Here are some tips for overcoming networking challenges as an introverted professional:

1. **Prepare in advance**: Before attending networking events, do your research on the attendees, companies, or industries that will be present. This preparation will give you a foundation for starting conversations and asking relevant questions, increasing your confidence and comfort level.
2. **Set achievable goals**: Instead of aiming to meet many people, focus on establishing a few meaningful connections. This approach can be more manageable and rewarding for introverts, as it allows for deeper conversations and more genuine connections.
3. **Arrive early**: Being one of the first attendees at an event can make it easier to initiate conversations, as people are more likely to be open to meeting new individuals before the room becomes crowded and noisy.
4. **Practice active listening**: Use your natural inclination for deep listening to your advantage during networking events. People appreciate being heard and understood, and your ability to listen attentively can help you create strong, lasting connections.
5. **Find common ground**: Look for shared interests, experiences, or challenges to connect with others on a deeper level. This can make the conversation more engaging and memorable for both parties, laying the foundation for a meaningful professional relationship.
6. **Leverage online networking**: Introverts may find it easier to network through online platforms, such as LinkedIn, industry-specific forums, or virtual networking events. This format can provide a more controlled environment, giving you the opportunity to engage in one-on-one conversations and share your thoughts and expertise more comfortably.
7. **Follow up**: After networking events, make a point to follow up with the people you connected with. A simple email or message expressing your appreciation for the conversation and your interest in staying connected can help solidify your new relationships.

8. **Focus on quality over quantity**: Remember that the goal of networking is not to amass many superficial connections, but to build a network of meaningful relationships that can provide support, mentorship, and opportunities for professional growth.

By embracing these strategies, introverted professionals can overcome the challenges of networking and leverage their unique qualities to create lasting, valuable connections. With preparation, persistence, and a focus on genuine connection, introverts can thrive in the networking arena and contribute to their professional success.

Building Authentic Connections

As an introvert, your natural inclination for deep thinking and genuine engagement can be a significant asset in building authentic connections. By prioritizing quality over quantity and focusing on the principles of trust, empathy, and mutual support, you can create meaningful relationships that enrich your personal and professional life. Here are some tips for building authentic connections:

1. **Be genuine**: When meeting new people, be true to yourself and let your authentic personality shine through. Avoid trying to impress others or conform to their expectations. Genuine connections are built on honesty and authenticity, so embrace your unique qualities and interests.
2. **Listen actively**: Make a conscious effort to listen deeply and attentively to others, demonstrating genuine interest in their thoughts, feelings, and experiences. This level of engagement can help create a strong foundation for meaningful relationships built on trust and understanding.
3. **Ask open-ended questions**: Encourage deeper conversations by asking open-ended questions that invite thoughtful responses. This approach can help you uncover shared interests, values, and experiences, providing a basis for authentic connections.
4. **Show empathy and understanding**: Strive to understand others' perspectives and emotions, even if they differ from your own. Demonstrating empathy and understanding can create an atmosphere of mutual respect and acceptance, fostering stronger connections.
5. **Be vulnerable**: Share your own experiences, challenges, and emotions with others, as vulnerability can help build trust and deepen connections. By opening and allowing others to see your authentic self, you invite them to do the same.
6. **Invest time and effort**: Building authentic connections requires time and effort. Make a point to maintain regular communication, schedule quality time together, and actively participate in each other's lives.

7. **Offer support**: Be a reliable source of support for your connections, providing encouragement, advice, or simply a listening ear when needed. This supportive environment can strengthen your relationships and create a sense of trust and security.
8. **Celebrate successes**: Acknowledge and celebrate the achievements and milestones of your connections. Demonstrating that you genuinely care about their happiness and well-being can help solidify your bonds and deepen your relationships.

By adopting these strategies, you can foster authentic connections that enrich your life and provide a strong support network. Embracing your introverted qualities and focusing on genuine engagement, empathy, and shared experiences can help you build lasting, meaningful relationships that withstand the test of time.

Utilizing Online Networking Opportunities

In today's digital age, online networking has become an increasingly important aspect of building personal and professional connections. For introverts, online networking can offer a more controlled and comfortable environment for engaging with others and establishing meaningful relationships. Here are some tips for effectively utilizing online networking opportunities:

1. **Optimize your online presence**: Make sure your online profiles (e.g., LinkedIn, professional website, or industry-specific platforms) accurately represent your skills, experiences, and interests. A well-crafted profile can help you make a strong first impression and attract like-minded connections.
2. **Join relevant groups or forums**: Seek out online communities related to your industry, interests, or goals. These groups can provide valuable resources, discussions, and networking opportunities tailored to your specific needs.
3. **Engage in meaningful conversations**: When participating in online discussions or forums, strive to contribute valuable insights, ask thoughtful questions, and share your expertise. This approach can help you build a reputation as a knowledgeable and engaged professional, attracting connections and opportunities.
4. **Build relationships through direct messaging**: If you come across individuals who share your interests or goals, reach out to them through direct messaging. Express your admiration for their work, ask for advice, or initiate a conversation about a shared interest. This personalized approach can lay the foundation for a genuine connection.

5. **Attend virtual networking events**: Participate in webinars, online workshops, or virtual conferences to expand your network and stay informed about industry trends. These events often include opportunities for networking, such as breakout sessions or chat features, where you can engage with fellow attendees in a more controlled environment.
6. **Follow up**: After connecting with someone online or attending a virtual event, follow up with a thoughtful message expressing your appreciation for the interaction and your interest in staying connected. This follow-up can help solidify the relationship and open the door for future collaborations or opportunities.
7. **Maintain your online relationships**: Just like in-person connections, online relationships require time and effort to maintain. Engage in regular communication, share relevant resources, and offer support or encouragement when needed. By investing in your online connections, you can cultivate strong, lasting relationships that transcend the digital realm.
8. **Balance online and offline networking**: While online networking offers unique advantages for introverts, it's important to also engage in face-to-face interactions when possible. Balancing online and offline networking can help you develop a well-rounded network and improve your overall communication skills.

By embracing these strategies, introverts can effectively utilize online networking opportunities to build valuable personal and professional connections. Leveraging digital platforms and virtual events can provide a comfortable environment for introverts to engage with others, share their expertise, and expand their network on their own terms.

Part III: Harnessing Your Introverted Power

Chapter 7: Unleashing Your Creativity: Introverts as Innovators

The Link Between Introversion and Creativity
Introverts are often associated with creativity and innovation, as their natural inclination for deep thinking, reflection, and solitude can foster an environment conducive to generating original ideas and solutions. This section will explore the link between introversion and creativity, highlighting the unique qualities that make introverts well-suited for innovation.

1. **The power of solitude**: Introverts tend to thrive in quiet, solitary environments, where they can process information and ideas without the distractions of external stimuli. This solitude allows introverts to delve deep into their thoughts and explore their inner world, often leading to the generation of creative ideas and insights.
2. **Deep focus**: Introverts are known for their ability to concentrate intensely on a particular task or subject for extended periods. This deep focus can help them explore complex problems and ideas, ultimately resulting in innovative solutions and creative breakthroughs.
3. **Introspection and self-awareness**: Introverts are naturally introspective, constantly examining their thoughts, emotions, and experiences. This heightened self-awareness can help them recognize patterns, draw connections, and generate unique insights that contribute to their creative output.
4. **Sensitivity to subtleties**: Introverts often have a keen eye for detail, noticing subtle cues and patterns that others may overlook. This attention to detail can help them identify creative opportunities and develop innovative solutions in various fields, from art and design to technology and science.

5. **Embracing complexity**: Introverts are generally comfortable with ambiguity and complexity, as their introspective nature allows them to explore multiple perspectives and ideas simultaneously. This ability to embrace complexity can lead to the generation of creative, nuanced solutions to challenging problems.
6. **Persistence and resilience**: Introverts may have a greater tolerance for the solitude and perseverance often required in the creative process. Their innate persistence and resilience can help them navigate the ups and downs of innovation, allowing them to stay committed to their creative pursuits despite setbacks or obstacles.

By understanding and leveraging these unique qualities, introverts can harness their creative potential and make significant contributions as innovators in various fields. Embracing their introverted nature and capitalizing on their strengths can help introverts thrive in the creative realm, ultimately leading to personal and professional success.

Cultivating Creative Habits and Environments

To fully unleash your creative potential as an introvert, it's essential to develop habits and create environments that foster creativity and innovation. Here are some strategies for cultivating creative habits and environments that can help you make the most of your introverted strengths:

1. **Prioritize solitude**: Schedule regular periods of solitude and quiet reflection in your daily routine. Use this time to process your thoughts, explore new ideas, or work on creative projects without the distractions of external stimuli.
2. **Develop a consistent routine**: Establishing a consistent daily routine can help you create a structure that supports your creative pursuits. Dedicate specific times for creative work, reflection, and relaxation, allowing yourself the space to think deeply and generate new ideas.
3. **Embrace curiosity**: Foster a mindset of curiosity and openness, actively seeking out new experiences, perspectives, and ideas. This can help expand your creative horizons and spark inspiration from unexpected sources.
4. **Practice mindfulness**: Incorporate mindfulness practices, such as meditation or journaling, into your routine to cultivate greater self-awareness and introspection. These practices can help you become more in tune with your thoughts and emotions, providing valuable insights that can inform your creative work.
5. **Create a conducive workspace**: Design a workspace that supports your creative needs and preferences as an introvert. This may include a quiet, private space where you can work without interruptions, as well as elements that promote focus and inspiration, such as comfortable furniture, calming colours, or inspirational artwork.

6. **Engage in creative exercises**: Regularly challenge yourself with creative exercises or prompts that push you to think outside the box and explore new ideas. This practice can help you develop your creative muscles and generate a constant stream of fresh ideas.
7. **Collaborate selectively**: While introverts often thrive in solitude, collaborating with like-minded individuals can provide valuable feedback, support, and inspiration. Choose your collaborators carefully, ensuring they share your values and respect your introverted nature.
8. **Take breaks and recharge**: As an introvert, it's essential to prioritize self-care and allow yourself time to recharge after periods of intense creative work or social interaction. Regular breaks and relaxation can help you maintain your energy levels and support your overall well-being.
9. **Reflect on your progress**: Regularly assess your creative goals, progress, and accomplishments, taking note of any patterns, strengths, or areas for improvement. This reflection can help you refine your creative process and stay motivated in your pursuits.

By cultivating these creative habits and environments, you can fully harness your introverted strengths and foster a more productive and innovative mindset. Embracing your unique qualities and creating an environment that supports your creative needs can help you thrive as an introvert in the world of innovation and imagination.

Leveraging Your Introverted Strengths in Creative Pursuits
As an introvert, your unique qualities can serve as powerful assets in your creative pursuits. By understanding and leveraging these strengths, you can overcome challenges, enhance your creative output, and make a lasting impact in your chosen field. Here are some strategies for leveraging your introverted strengths in creative pursuits:
1. **Capitalize on your deep focus**: Use your innate ability to concentrate on a single task or idea for extended periods to your advantage. By immersing yourself in your creative work, you can delve deeper into complex subjects and generate innovative ideas that set you apart from others.
2. **Harness the power of introspection**: Tap into your natural tendency for introspection and self-reflection to gain insights into your creative process, motivations, and challenges. This self-awareness can help you refine your approach, overcome obstacles, and develop a more authentic and unique creative voice.

3. **Utilize your empathy and listening skills**: Leverage your strong empathetic and listening abilities to understand the needs, emotions, and perspectives of your audience or clients. This understanding can help you create more resonant and impactful creative work that connects with others on a deeper level.
4. **Embrace your sensitivity to subtleties**: Use your keen attention to detail to identify patterns, nuances, and opportunities for innovation that others may overlook. This sensitivity can help you create more intricate, thoughtful, and original creative work.
5. **Apply your problem-solving abilities**: Draw on your natural problem-solving skills to approach creative challenges from unique angles, generating innovative solutions that differentiate your work from the competition.
6. **Develop your resilience**: Leverage your introverted resilience and persistence to stay committed to your creative pursuits, even when faced with setbacks or obstacles. This determination can help you overcome challenges and ultimately achieve your creative goals.
7. **Collaborate effectively**: While introverts may prefer to work alone, strategic collaboration can be invaluable in creative pursuits. Choose your collaborators wisely and develop a communication style that respects your introverted nature while fostering meaningful connections and productive collaboration.
8. **Seek feedback from trusted sources**: Introverts often benefit from soliciting feedback from a select group of trusted individuals who understand their creative vision and introverted nature. This feedback can provide valuable insights and guidance, helping you refine your work and grow as a creative professional.
9. **Emphasize your unique perspective**: As an introvert, your experiences and perspectives are inherently different from those of extroverts. Embrace this uniqueness and allow it to inform your creative work, resulting in a distinctive style or approach that sets you apart in your field.

By leveraging these introverted strengths, you can excel in your creative pursuits and make a lasting impact in your chosen field. Embracing your unique qualities and harnessing your natural abilities can help you achieve personal and professional success, while contributing to the world of innovation and creativity in a meaningful way.

Chapter 8: Developing Leadership Skills: How Introverts Can Excel as Leaders

Introverted Leadership Qualities
Contrary to popular belief, introverts can be highly effective leaders. Introverted leaders possess unique qualities that set them apart from their extroverted counterparts, and these strengths can be leveraged to excel in leadership roles. In this section, we will explore the key qualities that define introverted leadership and demonstrate how they contribute to successful leadership.

1. **Active listening and empathy**: Introverted leaders are natural listeners, giving them the ability to truly understand and empathize with their team members. This attentiveness enables them to connect with their team on a deeper level, fostering trust, rapport, and strong working relationships.
2. **Thoughtfulness and reflection**: Introverts tend to be thoughtful and reflective, carefully considering various aspects of a situation before making decisions. This approach can lead to more informed, strategic, and effective decision-making, which can greatly benefit the team and organization.
3. **Focus and persistence**: Introverted leaders have a strong ability to maintain focus on tasks and projects, and they're often dedicated to seeing them through to completion. This persistence can help drive the team forward and ensure that goals are met.
4. **Empowering team members**: Introverted leaders are more likely to delegate responsibilities and empower their team members, giving them the autonomy to make decisions and solve problems. This approach can lead to increased team engagement, motivation, and productivity.
5. **Creating inclusive environments**: Introverted leaders may be more sensitive to the needs and preferences of their team members, fostering an inclusive environment that accommodates various working styles, personalities, and perspectives. This inclusivity can result in a more cohesive, collaborative, and effective team.
6. **Leading by example**: Introverted leaders often lead by example, demonstrating their commitment to the team's goals and values through their actions and work ethic. This approach can inspire and motivate team members, while also establishing credibility and trust.

7. **Calmness under pressure**: Introverted leaders may remain calm and composed in high-pressure situations, providing a stabilizing presence for their team. This calm demeanour can help to diffuse tense situations and facilitate clear, rational decision-making.
8. **Valuing quality over quantity**: Introverted leaders may place a higher emphasis on the quality of their work and relationships, rather than focusing solely on achieving quantitative targets. This approach can lead to more sustainable and meaningful results for the team and organization.

By recognizing and embracing these introverted leadership qualities, introverts can excel in leadership roles and make a significant impact on their teams and organizations. Developing these strengths and leveraging them effectively can help introverts overcome stereotypes and demonstrate that they possess the skills, qualities, and potential to be successful leaders.

Effective Communication and Collaboration for Introverted Leaders

Communication and collaboration are essential skills for any leader, and introverted leaders can develop their own unique approaches to excel in these areas. Here are some strategies for introverted leaders to enhance their communication and collaboration skills:

1. **Embrace your listening skills**: As an introvert, you have a natural ability to listen actively and empathetically. Use this strength to engage in meaningful conversations, understand different perspectives, and build strong relationships with your team members.
2. **Develop your assertiveness**: While introverts may prefer a more reserved communication style, it's important to develop assertiveness when necessary. Practice being confident and clear in expressing your ideas, opinions, and expectations, while also respecting the viewpoints of others.
3. **Adapt your communication style**: Recognize that different team members may have different communication preferences. Be willing to adapt your communication style to suit the needs of others, whether that means engaging in one-on-one discussions, group meetings, or utilizing digital communication tools.
4. **Leverage written communication**: As an introvert, you might find it easier to express your thoughts and ideas in writing. Use this strength to communicate effectively through emails, memos, and other written channels, ensuring your message is clear, concise, and well-organized.
5. **Schedule regular check-ins**: Establish a routine of regular check-ins with your team members to discuss progress, address concerns, and provide feedback. This structure can help ensure open lines of communication and foster a collaborative environment.

6. **Create a collaborative culture**: Encourage collaboration among your team members by promoting an atmosphere of trust, respect, and inclusivity. Be receptive to feedback, ideas, and suggestions from your team, and empower them to take ownership of their work.
7. **Facilitate productive meetings**: As an introverted leader, you can create more effective meetings by setting clear objectives, encouraging participation from all attendees, and allowing time for reflection and discussion. Ensure that everyone's voice is heard and valued, and promote a balanced exchange of ideas.
8. **Utilize technology**: Make use of technology to facilitate communication and collaboration within your team. Digital tools such as project management software, video conferencing, and instant messaging can help streamline communication, encourage collaboration, and accommodate various working styles.
9. **Develop your non-verbal communication**: Pay attention to your body language, facial expressions, and tone of voice when communicating with others. These non-verbal cues can play a significant role in how your message is perceived and can help convey confidence, openness, and empathy.

By focusing on these strategies, introverted leaders can enhance their communication and collaboration skills, fostering strong, effective, and cohesive teams. Embracing your introverted strengths and adapting your approach to suit the needs of your team will enable you to excel as a leader and drive your team towards success.

Building and Managing Successful Teams: A Guide for Introverted Leaders

Building and managing successful teams is an essential skill for any leader, including introverts. Introverted leaders can leverage their unique strengths to create high-performing, collaborative, and engaged teams. Here are some strategies for introverted leaders to build and manage successful teams:

1. **Establish a clear vision and goals**: Clearly articulate your team's vision, objectives, and expectations. Make sure that all team members understand their roles, responsibilities, and how their work contributes to the overall success of the team.
2. **Hire for diversity and complementary skills**: When building your team, look for individuals with diverse backgrounds, perspectives, and skill sets. This diversity can foster creativity, innovation, and problem-solving, leading to better overall performance.
3. **Create an inclusive and supportive environment**: Encourage open communication, collaboration, and mutual respect among team members. Foster an inclusive environment where all perspectives are valued, and team members feel comfortable sharing their ideas, concerns, and feedback.

4. **Delegate and empower**: Delegate responsibilities to your team members, giving them the autonomy to make decisions and solve problems. This approach can increase engagement, motivation, and personal growth, leading to higher team performance.
5. **Provide regular feedback and support**: Offer constructive feedback, guidance, and support to help your team members grow and develop their skills. Schedule regular check-ins to discuss progress, address concerns, and celebrate achievements.
6. **Develop strong communication channels**: Establish clear, open, and effective communication channels within your team. Make use of various communication methods, such as face-to-face meetings, emails, and instant messaging, to accommodate different preferences and working styles.
7. **Promote collaboration and teamwork**: Encourage team members to work together, share ideas, and support each other. Foster a collaborative atmosphere by assigning team projects, organizing brainstorming sessions, and celebrating team accomplishments.
8. **Monitor progress and adjust as needed**: Regularly assess your team's progress toward its goals, and adjust as needed to ensure success. Identify any obstacles, challenges, or skill gaps, and address them promptly to keep your team on track.
9. **Invest in professional development**: Provide opportunities for team members to learn, grow, and develop their skills. Offer training, workshops, and mentoring programs to help your team members reach their full potential.
10. **Lead by example**: Model the behaviour and values you expect from your team members. Demonstrate your commitment to the team's success by actively participating, working hard, and treating others with respect and empathy.

By implementing these strategies, introverted leaders can effectively build and manage successful teams that are engaged, motivated, and high performing. By leveraging their unique strengths and creating an inclusive, supportive environment, introverted leaders can empower their teams to achieve their full potential and drive the organization's success.

Chapter 9: The Art of Public Speaking and Presentation for Introverts

Overcoming Fears of Public Speaking
Public speaking can be a daunting task for introverts, who may feel anxious or overwhelmed by the prospect of standing in front of an audience. However, with practice, preparation, and the right strategies, introverts can become confident and effective public speakers. Here are some tips for overcoming fears of public speaking as an introvert:

1. **Understand your fear**: Acknowledge and understand the sources of your anxiety around public speaking. Recognize that it is a common fear and that you are not alone in experiencing it. Identifying the root causes of your anxiety can help you develop targeted strategies for addressing it.
2. **Practice self-compassion**: Treat yourself with kindness and understanding, recognizing that it is normal to feel anxious or nervous about public speaking. Focus on your growth and progress, rather than expecting perfection.
3. **Prepare thoroughly**: Invest time and effort in preparing your speech or presentation. Familiarize yourself with the content, structure, and key points, so that you can deliver it confidently and fluently. Practicing your speech multiple times can help you feel more comfortable and in control.
4. **Develop a strong opening**: Craft a powerful and engaging opening that will grab the attention of your audience and set the tone for the rest of your presentation. This can help you feel more confident and in control from the outset.
5. **Focus on your message**: Remember that the purpose of your speech is to share your message, knowledge, or ideas with your audience. Concentrate on delivering your message clearly and effectively, rather than focusing on yourself or your fears.
6. **Breathe and relax**: Before taking the stage, practice deep breathing exercises and relaxation techniques to help calm your nerves and release tension. This can help you feel more centred and focused during your presentation.
7. **Visualize success**: Imagine yourself delivering a successful and well-received presentation. Visualization can help boost your confidence and reinforce a positive mindset.
8. **Embrace your introverted strengths**: Utilize your natural tendencies for deep thinking, reflection, and empathy to enhance your public speaking skills. Focus on crafting a thoughtful and well-researched presentation that demonstrates your expertise and connects with your audience.

9. **Seek support**: Share your fears and concerns with trusted friends, family members, or colleagues. They can offer encouragement, advice, and constructive feedback to help you improve your public speaking skills.
10. **Practice, practice, practice**: Like any skill, public speaking improves with practice. Seek out opportunities to practice your public speaking skills in low-stakes situations, such as local clubs, workshops, or small group presentations. This will help you gain experience and confidence over time.

By implementing these strategies and focusing on growth and progress, introverts can overcome their fears of public speaking and develop the skills to deliver powerful, engaging, and effective presentations.

Developing Effective Presentation Skills

Effective presentation skills are essential for success in many professional and personal settings. For introverts looking to enhance their public speaking abilities, here are some tips for developing impactful presentation skills:

1. **Know your audience**: Research and understand your audience's needs, interests, and expectations. Tailor your presentation to address their concerns and speak to their level of understanding. This helps ensure your message resonates and is well-received.
2. **Organize your content**: Structure your presentation logically and coherently, with a clear introduction, main points, and conclusion. Use headings, bullet points, and visual aids to highlight key ideas and make it easy for your audience to follow along.
3. **Use visual aids effectively**: Incorporate visual aids, such as slides, images, charts, and videos, to support and enhance your message. Be mindful of design principles, ensuring your visuals are clear, engaging, and relevant. Avoid overcrowding your slides with too much information or distracting elements.
4. **Engage your audience**: Encourage audience interaction and engagement by asking questions, soliciting opinions, and using interactive activities. This helps maintain interest and fosters a more dynamic and memorable presentation.
5. **Master your body language**: Be mindful of your posture, gestures, and facial expressions during your presentation. Adopt a confident and open posture, make eye contact, and use natural gestures to reinforce your message. Avoid fidgeting, crossing your arms, or looking down, as these can detract from your credibility and authority.
6. **Vary your tone and pace**: Use vocal variety to keep your audience engaged and maintain their attention. Adjust your tone, pitch, volume, and pace to emphasize key points and create interest. Avoid speaking in a monotone voice, which can quickly lose your audience's attention.

7. **Rehearse and refine**: Practice your presentation multiple times, focusing on your delivery, timing, and transitions between slides. This helps build your confidence and ensures you are well-prepared to deliver your message effectively.
8. **Handle questions and objections gracefully**: Anticipate potential questions or objections from your audience and prepare thoughtful responses. When faced with unexpected questions, take a moment to gather your thoughts before answering. Be respectful and open-minded, and acknowledge different perspectives or opinions.
9. **Manage your nerves**: Utilize relaxation techniques, such as deep breathing exercises, visualization, or mindfulness, to help calm your nerves before and during your presentation. Remember that it is normal to feel some anxiety, and focus on delivering your message with confidence and clarity.
10. **Evaluate and learn**: After your presentation, reflect on what went well and areas for improvement. Seek feedback from your audience or peers, and use this information to refine and enhance your presentation skills moving forward.

By applying these strategies and committing to ongoing practice and development, introverts can cultivate effective presentation skills that help them communicate their ideas and insights with confidence and impact.

Engaging and Connecting with Your Audience

Connecting with your audience is a crucial aspect of delivering a successful presentation. As an introvert, you can leverage your natural strengths, such as empathy and deep thinking, to engage and connect with your audience effectively. Here are some strategies for building rapport and fostering a genuine connection with your listeners:

1. **Research your audience**: Before your presentation, learn about your audience's background, interests, and needs. This will help you tailor your message and delivery to their expectations, ensuring that your content is relevant and engaging.
2. **Establish common ground**: Begin your presentation by identifying shared experiences, values, or concerns that resonate with your audience. This can create a sense of connection and trust, making your listeners more receptive to your message.
3. **Be genuine and authentic**: Speak from the heart and share personal stories, anecdotes, or insights that demonstrate your passion and expertise. This helps establish credibility and creates a more relatable and engaging presentation.
4. **Make eye contact**: Maintaining eye contact with your audience members helps establish a personal connection and demonstrates that you are genuinely interested in their thoughts and reactions.

5. **Use inclusive language**: Choose words and phrases that foster a sense of unity and belonging. For example, use "we" and "our" instead of "I" and "my" to create a sense of shared ownership and inclusivity.
6. **Ask open-ended questions**: Encourage audience participation and engagement by asking open-ended questions that invite their thoughts, opinions, or experiences. This can foster a more interactive and dynamic presentation, while also helping you better understand your audience's perspectives.
7. **Be responsive and adaptable**: Pay attention to audience cues, such as body language, facial expressions, and comments. Be prepared to adapt your content, pacing, or delivery based on their reactions, ensuring that your message remains relevant and engaging.
8. **Use humour appropriately**: Light-hearted jokes or anecdotes can help put your audience at ease and create a more relaxed atmosphere. However, be mindful of your audience's sensibilities and ensure that your humour is appropriate and inclusive.
9. **Show empathy and understanding**: Validate your audience's feelings, concerns, or experiences, demonstrating that you understand their perspectives and care about their well-being. This can help build trust and rapport, making it more likely that they will engage with and respond positively to your message.
10. **End on a high note**: Conclude your presentation with a powerful closing statement or call-to-action that leaves a lasting impression and motivates your audience to act or reflect on your message.

By applying these strategies and leveraging your introverted strengths, you can create a meaningful connection with your audience, resulting in a more engaging, memorable, and impactful presentation.

Part IV: Personal Growth and Self-Care

Chapter 10: Setting Boundaries: Protecting Your Energy and Well-Being

Identifying Personal Boundaries

Personal boundaries are crucial for maintaining a healthy sense of self and well-being, especially for introverts who may need more solitude and downtime to recharge. Identifying your personal boundaries involves recognizing and respecting your own limits, values, and needs. Here are some tips for identifying your personal boundaries:

1. **Reflect on your values**: Consider your core values and beliefs that guide your decisions and behaviours. These values can help you define what is acceptable and unacceptable in various aspects of your life, such as relationships, work, and social situations.
2. **Understand your emotional limits**: Identify the situations, people, or behaviours that cause you emotional distress or discomfort. Recognizing these emotional triggers can help you set boundaries that protect your emotional well-being.
3. **Acknowledge your physical boundaries**: Pay attention to your body's signals and needs, such as hunger, fatigue, or discomfort. Understand your personal space preferences and the level of physical touch that you feel comfortable with in different contexts.
4. **Consider your time and energy**: Reflect on your priorities, commitments, and energy levels. Determine how much time and effort you can realistically devote to various activities and relationships without sacrificing your well-being.
5. **Assess your social boundaries**: Evaluate your preferences for social interaction, such as the types of activities, group sizes, and environments that you feel most comfortable in. This can help you set boundaries that honour your introverted nature and support your social well-being.

6. **Identify your work-life balance**: Understand your limits when it comes to work and personal life. Recognize the importance of maintaining a balance between professional responsibilities and personal self-care, and set boundaries to protect this balance.
7. **Establish communication boundaries**: Determine your preferred methods and frequency of communication, both in personal relationships and professional settings. This can help you maintain a sense of control and autonomy over your interactions with others.

Once you have identified your personal boundaries, the next step is to communicate and enforce these boundaries with others. This can be challenging, but it is essential for protecting your energy, well-being, and personal growth as an introvert.

Communicating Boundaries Effectively

Effectively communicating your boundaries is essential for ensuring that others understand and respect your needs and limits. Here are some tips for communicating your boundaries assertively and respectfully:

1. **Be clear and specific**: Clearly state your boundaries in a straightforward and specific manner. Use concrete examples and descriptions to help others understand your limits and expectations.
2. **Use "I" statements**: Frame your boundaries in terms of your own feelings and needs, rather than making accusatory or blaming statements. This can help reduce defensiveness and promote understanding. For example, say, "I feel overwhelmed when I have too many social engagements in a week, so I need some alone time to recharge," instead of, "You always expect me to attend every event."
3. **Practice assertiveness**: Be firm and assertive when expressing your boundaries, without being aggressive or confrontational. Stand your ground and calmly reiterate your needs if others push back or try to cross your boundaries.
4. **Be consistent**: Consistently enforce your boundaries to reinforce their importance and help others understand that they need to be respected. This may require repetition and reinforcement over time, particularly if others are used to crossing your boundaries in the past.
5. **Offer alternatives**: When setting boundaries, consider offering alternatives or compromises that may help meet both your needs and the needs of others. This can demonstrate your willingness to collaborate and find a solution that works for everyone involved.
6. **Model respect**: Show respect for other people's boundaries and model the behaviour you expect from them. This can help create a more supportive and understanding environment where everyone's needs and limits are valued.

7. **Be prepared for resistance**: Understand that some people may resist or push back against your boundaries, particularly if they are not used to respecting them. Stay calm and assertive in the face of resistance, and remember that you have the right to set limits and protect your well-being.
8. **Revisit and adjust**: Regularly reassess your boundaries to ensure they continue to meet your needs and reflect your current circumstances. Be open to adjusting your boundaries as necessary, and communicate any changes to those affected.

By communicating your boundaries effectively, you can help create an environment where your needs and limits are respected, allowing you to protect your energy, well-being, and personal growth as an introvert.

Balancing Work, Social, and Personal Life

Achieving a balance between work, social, and personal life is crucial for maintaining overall well-being and happiness, especially for introverts who may need more solitude and downtime to recharge. Here are some tips for finding and maintaining balance in your life:

1. **Set priorities**: Determine what aspects of your life are most important to you and prioritize them accordingly. This might include work, relationships, health, hobbies, or personal development. Regularly reassess your priorities to ensure they align with your current needs and goals.
2. **Establish boundaries**: Set clear boundaries between different aspects of your life to prevent one area from consuming too much time and energy. This may involve setting limits on work hours, creating dedicated times for social activities, and carving out regular periods for personal self-care and reflection.
3. **Schedule downtime**: Plan regular periods of solitude and relaxation to recharge your energy, particularly after engaging in demanding social or work activities. This may involve incorporating daily or weekly self-care rituals, such as meditation, journaling, or engaging in hobbies that bring you joy.
4. **Develop a support network**: Cultivate strong relationships with friends, family, and colleagues who understand and respect your need for balance. Seek out like-minded individuals who share similar values and priorities, and who can provide encouragement and support in maintaining a balanced life.
5. **Be flexible**: Recognize that achieving balance is an ongoing process and may require adjustments over time. Be open to reassessing and reorganizing your life as your needs and circumstances change, and give yourself permission to adapt and evolve.

6. **Practice self-compassion**: Understand that achieving balance can be challenging, and it's normal to experience setbacks or imbalances from time to time. Be kind to yourself when things don't go as planned, and use setbacks as opportunities to learn and grow.
7. **Communicate your needs**: Openly discuss your needs and priorities with those around you, such as your partner, friends, or colleagues. This can help create a supportive environment where everyone's needs are respected, and it can foster collaboration in finding solutions that work for everyone involved.
8. **Prioritize self-care**: Make your well-being a priority by incorporating self-care activities into your daily routine. This may include exercise, proper nutrition, sufficient sleep, and engaging in activities that nourish your mind and soul.

By consciously focusing on finding balance between work, social, and personal life, you can ensure that your needs as an introvert are met, leading to a more fulfilling, happy, and healthy life.

Specific Actions or Exercises for Establishing Boundaries

Establishing boundaries is essential for maintaining a healthy and balanced life. Here are some specific actions and exercises to help you set and enforce boundaries:

1. **Reflect on your needs and values**: Take time to reflect on your personal needs, values, and priorities. Consider what aspects of your life require boundaries and what limits you need to set to protect your well-being.
2. **Identify potential boundary violations**: Make a list of situations or behaviours that make you feel uncomfortable or drained. These can include excessive work hours, constant social engagements, or people who frequently overstep your personal space.
3. **Develop clear and specific boundaries**: For each situation or behaviour you identified, develop clear and specific boundaries. Be as detailed as possible, outlining the limits and expectations you have for yourself and others.
4. **Practice assertive communication**: Learn and practice assertive communication techniques, such as using "I" statements, maintaining a calm and confident tone, and being direct and clear when expressing your boundaries.
5. **Role-play scenarios**: Practice setting boundaries by role-playing scenarios with a trusted friend or family member. This can help you become more comfortable with expressing your limits and handling potential resistance.
6. **Establish a self-care routine**: Create a self-care routine that supports your boundaries and helps you maintain balance. Schedule regular breaks and downtime to recharge, and prioritize activities that nourish your mind, body, and soul.

7. **Set consequences for boundary violations**: Establish consequences for instances when your boundaries are violated. This may involve limiting contact with individuals who consistently disrespect your limits or taking a step back from situations that continually push your boundaries.
8. **Reinforce your boundaries consistently**: Be consistent in enforcing your boundaries and communicating them to others. Remember that it may take time for people to adjust to your new limits, and consistency is key in helping them understand and respect your boundaries.
9. **Evaluate and adjust your boundaries**: Regularly reassess your boundaries to ensure they continue to meet your needs and reflect your current circumstances. Be open to adjusting your boundaries as necessary, and communicate any changes to those affected.
10. **Celebrate your successes**: Acknowledge and celebrate your successes in setting and maintaining boundaries. This can help build your confidence and reinforce the importance of boundaries in your life.

By implementing these specific actions and exercises, you can establish healthy boundaries that protect your well-being and create a balanced life.

Chapter 11: Practicing Mindfulness and Meditation: A Path to Inner Peace

The Benefits of Mindfulness and Meditation for Introverts
Mindfulness and meditation are practices that can provide numerous benefits for introverts, helping them cultivate inner peace, self-awareness, and emotional resilience. Here are some of the key advantages of incorporating mindfulness and meditation into your life as an introvert:

1. **Stress reduction**: Mindfulness and meditation have been shown to effectively reduce stress levels by helping you regulate your emotions, promoting relaxation, and increasing your ability to cope with daily challenges.
2. **Increased self-awareness**: As an introvert, you may already possess a natural inclination for introspection. Practicing mindfulness and meditation can enhance your self-awareness, helping you better understand your thoughts, emotions, and patterns of behaviour.
3. **Improved focus and concentration**: Meditation and mindfulness practices can help you develop greater focus and concentration, allowing you to engage more effectively in tasks and activities that require deep thought and reflection.
4. **Enhanced emotional resilience**: Mindfulness and meditation can help you cultivate emotional resilience by teaching you to observe your thoughts and feelings without judgment, enabling you to better manage stress, anxiety, and other emotional challenges.
5. **Better energy management**: As an introvert, you may find that social interactions and external stimulation can be draining. Mindfulness and meditation practices can help you become more attuned to your energy levels and develop strategies for conserving and replenishing your energy as needed.
6. **Increased self-compassion**: Mindfulness and meditation can help you cultivate self-compassion, allowing you to be kinder and more forgiving towards yourself. This can be especially beneficial for introverts, who may experience self-doubt or criticism due to societal expectations or misconceptions about introversion.
7. **Deeper connection with others**: Although introverts may prefer fewer, more meaningful relationships, mindfulness and meditation can enhance your ability to connect with others on a deeper level by fostering empathy, compassion, and active listening skills.

8. **Personal growth**: Mindfulness and meditation practices can encourage personal growth by prompting you to explore your inner thoughts, emotions, and beliefs. As an introvert, you may find that these practices align well with your natural inclination for self-reflection and introspection.

By incorporating mindfulness and meditation into your daily routine, you can tap into these benefits and create a more balanced, peaceful, and fulfilling life as an introvert.

Different Meditation Techniques

There are various meditation techniques to choose from, each with its unique approach and benefits. Here are some popular meditation techniques that you may want to explore:

1. **Mindfulness Meditation**: This technique involves focusing on the present moment and accepting it without judgment. You can practice mindfulness meditation by paying attention to your breath, bodily sensations, thoughts, or external sounds, while maintaining a non-judgmental awareness of your experience.
2. **Concentration Meditation**: This form of meditation requires you to focus your attention on a single point, such as your breath, a mantra, or a visual object. The goal is to train your mind to maintain unwavering attention on the chosen focal point, thereby improving your concentration and mental stability.
3. **Loving-Kindness Meditation (Metta Meditation)**: This technique focuses on cultivating feelings of love, compassion, and goodwill towards yourself and others. It typically involves silently repeating phrases, such as "May I be happy, may I be healthy, may I be safe," and then extending these well-wishes to others, including loved ones, acquaintances, and even those you may have conflicts with.
4. **Body Scan Meditation**: Also known as progressive muscle relaxation, this technique involves mentally scanning your body from head to toe, noting any areas of tension or discomfort, and consciously releasing the tension through relaxation or gentle movement.
5. **Transcendental Meditation**: This technique involves the repetition of a specific mantra, which is assigned to you by a certified teacher. You silently repeat the mantra in your mind during meditation sessions, allowing your thoughts to naturally come and go while maintaining your focus on the mantra.
6. **Guided Meditation**: In this form of meditation, you are guided through a series of mental images, visualizations, or scenarios by a narrator or recording. The goal is to help you cultivate a sense of relaxation, inner peace, or personal growth using vivid mental imagery.

7. **Yoga Nidra**: Also known as yogic sleep, this technique involves lying down in a comfortable position and following a series of guided instructions that lead you through different stages of deep relaxation and self-inquiry, ultimately reaching a state of conscious awareness between wakefulness and sleep.
8. **Walking Meditation**: This practice combines mindfulness with physical movement, as you walk slowly and deliberately while maintaining a focus on your breath, bodily sensations, or the movement of your feet.
9. **Zen Meditation (Zazen)**: In this technique, practiced in the Zen Buddhist tradition, you sit in a specific posture, usually on a cushion or a chair, and focus on your breath as it moves in and out of your body. The goal is to cultivate a sense of alertness, presence, and equanimity.
10. **Vipassana Meditation**: Also known as insight meditation, this technique involves observing your thoughts, emotions, and bodily sensations with a non-judgmental attitude, cultivating a deep understanding of the impermanent nature of experiences and the interconnectedness of all things.

These are just a few examples of the many meditation techniques available. You may wish to try several of these methods to find the one that resonates best with you and aligns with your personal goals and preferences.

Incorporating Mindfulness into Daily Life

Mindfulness is the practice of being fully present in the moment, with a non-judgmental awareness of your thoughts, feelings, and sensations. By incorporating mindfulness into your daily life, you can cultivate greater self-awareness, reduce stress, and improve your overall well-being. Here are some tips for integrating mindfulness into your everyday routine:

1. **Start with the breath**: Begin by taking a few deep, conscious breaths throughout the day, focusing on the sensation of your breath as it enters and leaves your body. This simple act can help you become more aware of your present experience and anchor your attention in the here and now.
2. **Practice mindful eating**: During meals, slow down and savour each bite, paying attention to the taste, texture, and aroma of your food. Try to eat without distractions, such as watching TV or scrolling through your phone, to fully engage with the experience of eating.
3. **Mindful walking**: Whether you're walking to work or taking a leisurely stroll, practice mindful walking by focusing on the sensation of your feet hitting the ground and the rhythm of your steps. Observe your surroundings, taking in the sights, sounds, and smells around you.

4. **Mindful listening**: When conversing with others, practice active listening by giving your full attention to the speaker. Avoid interrupting or planning your response while they're talking; instead, focus on their words, tone of voice, and body language.
5. **Set mindfulness reminders**: Schedule regular mindfulness breaks throughout the day, using a timer or an app to remind you to pause and check in with yourself. During these breaks, take a few deep breaths and observe your thoughts, feelings, and physical sensations without judgment.
6. **Body awareness**: Periodically throughout the day, scan your body for any areas of tension or discomfort. Consciously relax those areas and adjust your posture if needed. This practice can help you become more in tune with your body's needs and signals.
7. **Mindful chores**: Turn everyday tasks, such as washing dishes or folding laundry, into mindfulness practices by focusing on the sensations, movements, and sounds involved in each activity. This can help transform mundane chores into moments of presence and awareness.
8. **Gratitude practice**: Cultivate gratitude by reflecting on the positive aspects of your life, such as supportive relationships, personal achievements, or simple pleasures. You can keep a gratitude journal or simply take a few moments each day to silently express appreciation for the good things in your life.
9. **Meditate**: Establish a regular meditation practice to deepen your mindfulness skills. You can start with just a few minutes a day and gradually increase the duration as you become more comfortable with the practice.
10. **Be patient and compassionate**: Developing mindfulness takes time and consistent practice. Remember to be patient with yourself and approach your efforts with self-compassion, recognizing that it's normal to experience challenges and setbacks along the way.

By integrating mindfulness into your daily life, you can cultivate greater self-awareness, reduce stress, and enhance your overall well-being. Remember, the key to success is consistency and patience, so give yourself the time and space to grow in your mindfulness practice.

Expert Opinions and Research Findings on Mindfulness and Introversion

1. **Dr. Jon Kabat-Zinn**: As the founder of the Mindfulness-Based Stress Reduction (MBSR) program, Dr. Jon Kabat-Zinn has conducted extensive research on the benefits of mindfulness. His studies have shown that mindfulness can help reduce stress, anxiety, and depression, and improve overall mental well-being. For introverts, mindfulness can help them manage their inner thoughts and emotions, as well as cope with overstimulation and social anxiety.

2. **Dr. Elaine Aron**: A psychologist and author of "The Highly Sensitive Person," Dr. Elaine Aron has researched the concept of sensory processing sensitivity, which is often associated with introversion. She suggests that practicing mindfulness can help highly sensitive individuals, including introverts, better manage their heightened sensitivity to external stimuli, improve emotional regulation, and enhance self-awareness.
3. **Dr. Susan Cain**: The author of the bestselling book "Quiet: The Power of Introverts in a World That Can't Stop Talking," Dr. Susan Cain advocates for the unique strengths and contributions of introverts. She highlights the importance of embracing one's introverted nature and using mindfulness as a tool to better understand and navigate the challenges that introverts may face in an extroverted world.
4. **Dr. Daniel Goleman**: A renowned psychologist and author of "Emotional Intelligence," Dr. Daniel Goleman emphasizes the importance of mindfulness in developing emotional intelligence. He argues that introverts can benefit from mindfulness practices, as they can help improve self-awareness, empathy, and emotional regulation—key components of emotional intelligence.
5. **Research on mindfulness-based interventions**: Numerous studies have demonstrated the effectiveness of mindfulness-based interventions, such as MBSR and Mindfulness-Based Cognitive Therapy (MBCT), in reducing stress, anxiety, and depression. These interventions have been shown to benefit a wide range of individuals, including introverts, by promoting emotional well-being and resilience.
6. **Research on mindfulness and the brain**: Neuroscientific research has found that mindfulness practices can lead to structural and functional changes in the brain, particularly in areas associated with attention, emotional regulation, and self-awareness. These findings suggest that introverts can benefit from mindfulness practices by enhancing their cognitive and emotional processing abilities.

In summary, expert opinions and research findings underscore the benefits of mindfulness for introverts. By incorporating mindfulness practices into their daily lives, introverts can improve their self-awareness, emotional regulation, and coping strategies in an extroverted world.

Chapter 12: Building Confidence and Overcoming Self-Doubt

Identifying and Challenging Limiting Beliefs
As an introvert, you may experience self-doubt and lack confidence in certain situations, especially when faced with social or professional challenges. These feelings can be fuelled by limiting beliefs – negative thoughts about yourself that hold you back from reaching your full potential. In this section, we'll explore strategies for identifying and challenging these limiting beliefs.

1. **Recognize your limiting beliefs**: Start by reflecting on the thoughts and beliefs that might be holding you back. These could be thoughts like "I'm not good enough," "I'm too shy," or "I can't succeed in social situations." Write down these beliefs and consider how they may be influencing your actions and decisions.
2. **Determine the source**: Once you've identified your limiting beliefs, consider where they might have originated. This could be from past experiences, messages from others, or societal expectations. Understanding the source of these beliefs can help you to challenge their validity and change your perspective.
3. **Gather evidence**: To challenge your limiting beliefs, gather evidence that contradicts them. For example, if you believe you're not good at public speaking, think about instances where you've successfully presented or spoken in front of others. Look for examples that demonstrate your abilities and strengths, and use these to counteract your negative beliefs.
4. **Reframe your beliefs**: Replace your limiting beliefs with more positive, empowering statements. For instance, instead of thinking "I'm too shy to make friends," you could reframe this belief as "I may be introverted, but I can still form deep, meaningful connections with others." Practice repeating these positive affirmations to yourself, and over time, they can help shift your mindset and boost your confidence.
5. **Challenge negative self-talk**: When negative thoughts arise, be aware of your internal dialogue and make a conscious effort to challenge these thoughts. Ask yourself if the thought is based on facts or assumptions, and consider alternative explanations or perspectives. This can help you develop a more balanced and realistic view of yourself and your abilities.
6. **Set achievable goals**: Break down your goals into smaller, more manageable steps, and celebrate your progress along the way. This can help build your confidence and reinforce your belief in your ability to achieve your objectives.

7. **Seek support**: Surround yourself with supportive people who believe in you and encourage your growth. Share your struggles with friends, family, or a therapist who can help you challenge your limiting beliefs and provide guidance on your journey to self-confidence.

By identifying and challenging your limiting beliefs, you can begin to overcome self-doubt and build confidence in your abilities as an introvert. Remember, confidence is a skill that can be developed over time, so be patient with yourself and continue practicing these strategies to foster growth and self-assurance.

Developing a Positive Self-Image
A positive self-image is crucial for building confidence, overcoming self-doubt, and maintaining overall well-being. As an introvert, it's essential to cultivate a healthy self-image that reflects your unique qualities and strengths. Here are some strategies to help you develop a positive self-image:

1. **Embrace your introverted nature**: Acknowledge and appreciate your introverted qualities, such as deep thinking, empathy, and creativity. Recognize that introversion is not a flaw, but rather a natural and valuable trait that contributes to your individuality and success.
2. **Focus on your strengths**: Identify your strengths and accomplishments, and remind yourself of these regularly. Make a list of your talents, skills, and achievements, and review this list whenever you need a self-esteem boost.
3. **Practice self-compassion**: Treat yourself with the same kindness and understanding you would offer a friend. Recognize that everyone makes mistakes and experiences setbacks, and use these opportunities for learning and growth rather than self-criticism.
4. **Challenge negative thoughts**: When negative thoughts about yourself arise, practice challenging and reframing these thoughts with more balanced and positive perspectives. Remember that your thoughts are not always accurate reflections of reality, and strive to develop a more objective and constructive inner dialogue.
5. **Set realistic expectations**: Avoid setting unrealistic standards for yourself, as this can lead to feelings of failure and disappointment. Instead, establish achievable goals and celebrate your progress, no matter how small.
6. **Cultivate gratitude**: Practice gratitude by regularly reflecting on the positive aspects of your life and the things you're thankful for. This can help shift your focus away from self-criticism and toward appreciation and contentment.

7. **Surround yourself with positive influences**: Spend time with people who uplift and encourage you, and distance yourself from those who undermine your self-image. Seek out friends, family members, and mentors who support your growth and value your unique qualities.
8. **Engage in self-care**: Prioritize your physical, emotional, and mental well-being by engaging in activities that nourish and recharge you. This could include exercise, healthy eating, meditation, hobbies, or spending time in nature.
9. **Develop a growth mindset**: Embrace the idea that you can learn, grow, and improve over time. View challenges and setbacks as opportunities for growth and development, and maintain a positive attitude toward self-improvement.

By consistently practicing these strategies, you can develop a positive self-image that reflects your true worth and potential as an introvert. Remember that building a healthy self-image is a lifelong journey, so be patient with yourself and continue to invest in your personal growth and well-being.

Celebrating Personal Achievements

Recognizing and celebrating your personal achievements is essential for boosting self-confidence, developing a positive self-image, and maintaining motivation. As an introvert, it's crucial to take the time to acknowledge your accomplishments and reward yourself for your hard work. Here are some tips for celebrating your personal achievements:

1. **Keep a success journal**: Document your accomplishments, both big and small, in a dedicated journal. Regularly writing down your achievements can help reinforce your successes and provide a visual reminder of your progress over time.
2. **Share your achievements**: Don't hesitate to share your accomplishments with friends, family, or colleagues. Letting others know about your successes can enhance your sense of accomplishment and provide an opportunity for others to celebrate with you.
3. **Set milestones**: Break down larger goals into smaller, more manageable milestones. When you reach a milestone, take the time to celebrate your progress and reflect on the effort and determination that led you to that point.
4. **Reward yourself**: Treat yourself to something special when you achieve a goal or milestone. This could be as simple as enjoying a favourite meal, watching a movie, or indulging in a relaxing activity. By rewarding yourself, you create positive associations with your achievements and reinforce the value of your hard work.

5. **Reflect on your growth**: Take a moment to reflect on how far you've come in your personal or professional journey. Consider the obstacles you've overcome, the skills you've developed, and the progress you've made. Acknowledging your growth can help you maintain a positive self-image and motivate you to continue striving for success.
6. **Practice gratitude**: Develop an attitude of gratitude by recognizing and appreciating the support and opportunities that have contributed to your achievements. Expressing gratitude can enhance your feelings of accomplishment and help you maintain a positive outlook on your successes.
7. **Display your achievements**: Find ways to visually display your accomplishments, whether that's a certificate on the wall, a trophy on the shelf, or a digital portfolio showcasing your work. Having tangible reminders of your achievements can serve as a constant source of motivation and pride.
8. **Pay it forward**: Celebrate your achievements by sharing your knowledge, experience, or resources with others. Mentoring, volunteering, or offering support to those in need can help you feel even more fulfilled and proud of your accomplishments.

By regularly acknowledging and celebrating your personal achievements, you can boost your self-esteem, stay motivated, and continue to grow and excel in your personal and professional life. Remember, every accomplishment, no matter how small, deserves recognition and celebration.

Specific Actions or Exercises for Boosting Self-Esteem

Boosting self-esteem requires consistent effort and practice. Here are some specific actions and exercises that can help you build and maintain a healthy sense of self-worth:

1. **Positive affirmations**: Develop a list of positive affirmations that resonate with you, and recite them daily. These affirmations should focus on your strengths, qualities, and achievements. Over time, these positive statements can help counteract negative self-talk and improve your self-esteem.
2. **Visualize success**: Spend a few minutes each day visualizing yourself achieving your goals and experiencing success. This mental rehearsal can help increase your self-confidence and motivation to pursue your objectives.
3. **Set realistic goals**: Establish achievable and measurable goals that align with your values and passions. As you work towards these goals and experience success, your self-esteem will naturally improve.
4. **Challenge negative thoughts**: Whenever you notice negative thoughts about yourself, practice questioning and reframing them with more balanced and positive perspectives. This cognitive restructuring can help you develop a healthier self-image.

5. **Celebrate achievements**: Regularly acknowledge and celebrate your accomplishments, both big and small. This can help reinforce your sense of self-worth and remind you of your capabilities.
6. **Practice self-compassion**: Treat yourself with kindness, understanding, and forgiveness, just as you would a close friend. Cultivating self-compassion can help you develop a more supportive and nurturing relationship with yourself.
7. **Engage in activities you enjoy**: Participate in hobbies and activities that bring you joy and a sense of accomplishment. This can help improve your mood, reduce stress, and enhance your self-esteem.
8. **Seek social support**: Surround yourself with positive, supportive individuals who uplift and encourage you. Having a strong support network can help you feel more valued and confident in your abilities.
9. **Develop assertiveness**: Practice expressing your thoughts, feelings, and needs in a clear and respectful manner. As your assertiveness improves, so will your self-esteem.
10. **Physical activity**: Regular exercise can have a positive impact on your self-esteem by reducing stress, improving mood, and increasing feelings of self-efficacy.
11. **Meditation and mindfulness**: Incorporate meditation and mindfulness practices into your daily routine. This can help you cultivate greater self-awareness, self-acceptance, and self-compassion, all of which contribute to a healthier self-esteem.

By consistently practicing these actions and exercises, you can gradually boost your self-esteem and develop a more positive and resilient sense of self-worth. Remember that building self-esteem is a lifelong journey, and it's essential to be patient and compassionate with yourself as you work towards this goal.

Part V: Creating an Introvert-Friendly Environment

Chapter 13: Designing Your Personal Sanctuary: Creating Spaces that Nurture Your Soul

Identifying Your Ideal Environment
Creating an introvert-friendly environment starts with identifying your ideal living space that caters to your unique needs and preferences. This personal sanctuary should provide you with a sense of comfort, safety, and inspiration. Consider the following steps when identifying your ideal environment:

1. **Assess your needs**: Reflect on the activities and elements that make you feel relaxed, energized, and focused. Consider how much quiet time and personal space you need to recharge and be productive.
2. **Prioritize comfort**: Ensure your personal sanctuary offers a comfortable and cosy atmosphere. This may involve having a comfortable seating area, warm lighting, or soft textures that make the space inviting and relaxing.
3. **Create a functional space**: Design your sanctuary with functionality in mind, taking into consideration the activities you typically engage in when seeking solace or focus. This might include a designated area for reading, writing, meditation, or creative pursuits.
4. **Incorporate nature**: Bring elements of nature into your personal sanctuary, such as plants, natural light, or a view of the outdoors. Studies have shown that exposure to nature can improve mental well-being and reduce stress.
5. **Choose a soothing colour palette**: Select colours that promote relaxation and tranquillity. Soft, muted colours or earth tones can create a calming atmosphere and contribute to a sense of serenity.

6. **Minimize distractions**: Design your space to minimize noise and visual distractions. This may involve using soundproofing materials, curtains, or partitions to create a sense of privacy and separation.
7. **Personalize your space**: Decorate your sanctuary with items that have personal significance or bring you joy. This could include artwork, photographs, or mementos that remind you of your accomplishments and cherished memories.
8. **Maintain order and cleanliness**: Keep your personal sanctuary clutter-free and organized, as a tidy environment can contribute to a sense of calm and focus.

By identifying your ideal environment and incorporating these elements into your personal sanctuary, you can create a space that nurtures your soul, provides an escape from external stimuli, and supports your introverted nature.

Creating a peaceful and comfortable living space

Creating a peaceful and comfortable living space is essential for your well-being, especially for introverts who require a sanctuary to recharge and decompress. Here are some tips to help you design a serene and cosy environment:

1. **Declutter and organize**: A clutter-free space promotes relaxation and reduces stress. Regularly declutter and organize your living space, keeping only items that serve a purpose or bring joy.
2. **Choose a calming colour palette**: opt for soothing colours that promote tranquillity and relaxation, such as soft blues, greens, greys, or earth tones.
3. **Incorporate natural elements**: Bring nature indoors by adding plants, natural materials (like wood or stone), or artwork depicting nature scenes. These elements can help create a more calming and inviting atmosphere.
4. **Optimize lighting**: Make use of natural light whenever possible and choose warm, ambient lighting for evenings. Consider using dimmer switches or lamps with adjustable brightness to create a cosy atmosphere.
5. **Focus on comfort**: Invest in comfortable furniture and soft furnishings, such as plush cushions, cosy blankets, and supportive seating options.
6. **Create designated spaces**: Designate specific areas for different activities, such as a reading nook, meditation corner, or workspace. This helps to create a sense of order and intentionality within your living space.
7. **Incorporate calming scents**: Use essential oils, candles, or incense to infuse your space with calming fragrances, such as lavender, chamomile, or sandalwood.

8. **Minimize noise**: Use rugs, curtains, or soundproofing materials to dampen noise and create a more peaceful environment. You might also consider using a white noise machine or soft background music to mask unwanted sounds.
9. **Personalize your space**: Decorate with items that have personal significance, evoke positive memories, or simply bring you joy. Surrounding yourself with meaningful objects can contribute to a sense of comfort and belonging.
10. **Establish a routine**: Create and maintain a daily routine that includes regular cleaning, organizing, and self-care activities. This consistency can help promote a peaceful and comfortable living space over time.

By implementing these tips, you can create a peaceful and comfortable living space that nurtures your well-being and supports your introverted nature, allowing you to thrive and recharge effectively.

Establishing Routines

Establishing routines is an essential aspect of maintaining a balanced and productive life. Routines can provide structure, reduce stress, and help you prioritize self-care. Here are some steps to help you establish effective routines:

1. **Identify your priorities**: Determine the key aspects of your life that you want to focus on, such as work, relationships, health, and personal growth. This will help you set goals and allocate time for activities that are important to you.
2. **Start small**: Begin by establishing one or two small routines that you can easily incorporate into your daily life. This could include a morning routine, an evening wind-down ritual, or a regular exercise regimen.
3. **Schedule your routines**: Allocate specific times of the day for your routines and create reminders or calendar events to help you stay consistent.
4. **Be realistic**: Set attainable goals for your routines, considering your current commitments, energy levels, and personal preferences. It's better to establish a simple, sustainable routine than to attempt something overly ambitious and become overwhelmed.
5. **Create a morning routine**: A well-structured morning routine can set the tone for the rest of the day. Consider incorporating activities such as stretching, meditation, journaling, or a healthy breakfast.
6. **Develop an evening routine**: Establish a calming evening routine to help you unwind and prepare for a restful night's sleep. This might include reading, taking a warm bath, or practicing gentle yoga.

7. **Incorporate self-care**: Make time for self-care activities within your routines, such as exercise, relaxation techniques, or hobbies that bring you joy.
8. **Stay flexible**: Life is unpredictable, and it's essential to remain adaptable when unexpected events disrupt your routines. Be willing to adjust your schedule and routines as needed to accommodate changes in your life.
9. **Track your progress**: Keep a log or journal to monitor your progress and reflect on the effectiveness of your routines. This can help you identify areas for improvement and celebrate your successes.
10. **Stay consistent**: Consistency is key to establishing and maintaining routines. Practice your routines regularly, and over time, they will become ingrained habits that contribute to a balanced and productive life.

By following these steps, you can establish routines that support your well-being, promote personal growth, and help you navigate life's challenges with greater ease and resilience.

Real-life examples of introvert-friendly spaces

Real-life examples of introvert-friendly spaces can provide inspiration for creating your own personal sanctuary. Here are a few examples of spaces designed with introverts in mind:

1. **Cosy reading nooks**: A small corner of a room can be transformed into a cosy reading nook with a comfortable chair, soft lighting, and a collection of your favourite books. This space offers a quiet refuge for introverts to indulge in their love of reading and escape from the hustle and bustle of daily life.
2. **Meditation spaces**: A dedicated meditation space, either indoors or outdoors, can provide a serene environment for introverts to practice mindfulness and self-reflection. These spaces often feature calming colours, natural elements, and minimal distractions to create a peaceful atmosphere conducive to relaxation.
3. **Home offices**: A well-designed home office can offer introverts a private and quiet space to focus on work or personal projects. Essential elements of an introvert-friendly home office include a comfortable desk, ergonomic chair, and organized storage solutions.
4. **Creative studios**: Introverts can benefit from a dedicated space to engage in creative pursuits, such as painting, writing, or crafting. A well-lit room with ample storage, inspiring artwork, and comfortable seating can foster creativity and provide a sanctuary for introverted artists.

5. **Garden retreats**: An outdoor space, such as a garden or patio, can serve as an introvert-friendly retreat where individuals can connect with nature, tend to plants, or simply relax in a peaceful setting. Comfortable seating, soothing water features, and fragrant plants can enhance the appeal of these spaces.
6. **Quiet cafes**: Some cafes cater to introverts by offering a quiet and comfortable atmosphere for patrons to enjoy a warm beverage, read, or work on their laptops. These establishments may feature soft lighting, comfortable seating, and a noise level that encourages quiet conversation or focused work.
7. **Introvert-friendly coworking spaces**: Coworking spaces can also cater to introverts by providing private workspaces, quiet zones, or designated areas for focused work. These facilities often balance the need for social interaction with the requirement for solitude and concentration.
8. **Nature retreats**: Many introverts find solace in natural settings, such as parks, forests, or beaches. These spaces allow introverts to recharge by connecting with nature, engaging in outdoor activities, or simply enjoying the peaceful surroundings.

By examining these real-life examples of introvert-friendly spaces, you can gather ideas and inspiration for creating your own personal sanctuary that supports your introverted nature and promotes well-being.

Chapter 14: The Future of Introversion: Embracing a New Social Paradigm

The rise of remote work and its benefits for introverts

The rise of remote work has been a boon for introverts, allowing them to work in environments that are conducive to their strengths and preferences. In this chapter, we'll explore the benefits of remote work for introverts and how it's shaping the future of work and social interaction.

Benefits of remote work for introverts:
- More control over work environment and schedule
- Reduction in distractions and interruptions
- Ability to work independently and autonomously
- Increased productivity and creativity
- Less stress and anxiety associated with social interaction in traditional office environments

The impact of remote work on social interaction:
- Decreased need for face-to-face interaction in the workplace
- Increased reliance on technology and virtual communication
- Greater emphasis on communication skills and collaboration in remote teams
- Shift towards more flexible and adaptive work arrangements

The role of introverts in shaping the future of work and social interaction:
- Embracing remote work and flexible work arrangements as a means of maximizing productivity and well-being
- Championing the benefits of introverted leadership qualities in a changing work landscape
- Advocating for a more inclusive and empathetic approach to social interaction and communication in the workplace and beyond

Through exploring the rise of remote work and its impact on social interaction, this chapter aims to provide insight and inspiration for introverts navigating a rapidly changing world. By embracing new opportunities and advocating for a more introvert-friendly approach to work and social interaction, introverts can thrive and contribute to a more empathetic and collaborative society.

The evolving role of introverts in society

Introverts have played an important role in society throughout history, but their impact is becoming increasingly visible in the modern world. In this chapter, we'll explore the evolving role of introverts in society and how their unique strengths and perspectives are shaping the world we live in.

The rise of introverted leaders:
- The changing nature of work has led to a greater appreciation for introverted leadership qualities such as empathy, listening skills, and thoughtfulness.
- Introverted leaders are increasingly sought after in industries such as technology and healthcare where collaboration, creativity, and problem-solving are essential.
- Research shows that introverted leaders can be just as effective, if not more so, than extroverted leaders, particularly in complex and uncertain environments.

The impact of introverts on culture and the arts:
- Introverts have made significant contributions to literature, music, and the visual arts throughout history.
- With the rise of social media and digital platforms, introverts have been able to reach wider audiences and share their creative work in new and innovative ways.
- The popularity of introvert-themed books, podcasts, and events demonstrates the growing cultural influence of introverts.

The importance of introverted perspectives in social and political issues:
- Introverts often approach social and political issues with a unique perspective, emphasizing empathy, listening, and critical thinking.
- The Me Too and Black Lives Matter movements are examples of social movements that have been driven in part by introverted voices and perspectives.
- Introverts are increasingly engaging in activism and advocacy through online platforms and other digital media.

As introverts continue to make their mark on society, it's important to recognize and appreciate their contributions. By valuing introverted leadership qualities, embracing diverse perspectives, and promoting empathy and collaboration, we can create a more inclusive and supportive society for all.

Imagining a more inclusive future for introverts and extroverts

As we continue to navigate a rapidly changing world, it's important to envision a future that embraces and celebrates the diversity of introverts and extroverts. In this final chapter, we'll explore the possibilities for a more inclusive future and how we can work towards creating a world that values and supports all personality types.

Creating work environments that accommodate introverts and extroverts:
- The rise of remote work and flexible work arrangements has provided new opportunities for introverts to work in environments that suit their strengths and preferences.
- Employers can create more inclusive work environments by offering a range of work arrangements and designing office spaces that cater to both introverted and extroverted employees.
- Embracing a culture of open communication and empathy can foster understanding and collaboration between introverted and extroverted team members.

Promoting empathy and understanding in personal relationships:
- Recognizing and respecting differences in personality type can improve communication and understanding in personal relationships.
- Developing a mutual understanding of each other's needs and preferences can help introverts and extroverts build stronger and more fulfilling relationships.
- Being open to trying new activities and experiences can expand both introverted and extroverted individuals' comfort zones and create new opportunities for connection and growth.

Encouraging a more inclusive and diverse society:
- Recognizing the value and strengths of introverts and extroverts can promote a more inclusive and diverse society.
- Supporting organizations and initiatives that prioritize diversity and inclusion can create new opportunities for introverts and extroverts to connect and collaborate.
- Embracing a culture of empathy and understanding can promote a more peaceful and harmonious society.

By imagining a more inclusive future for introverts and extroverts, we can work towards creating a world that values and supports individuals of all personality types. Through empathy, understanding, and collaboration, we can build stronger, more fulfilling personal relationships and create a more harmonious and inclusive society.

Conclusion: Your Introverted Journey - Embracing Your True Self and Thriving on Your Own Terms A concise summary of the key takeaways and actionable steps from each chapter Reinforcing the main points and providing a valuable reference for readers

Congratulations on completing your journey to embracing your introverted nature and thriving on your own terms. Throughout this book, we've explored the unique strengths and challenges of introverts and provided practical strategies and actionable steps to help you navigate social situations, build meaningful connections, and harness your introverted power.

In Part I, we debunked common myths about introversion and explored the science behind introversion and how it impacts the way we process information and interact with the world.

In Part II, we provided strategies for navigating social situations and building strong relationships, including tips for networking and developing leadership skills.

In Part III, we explored the power of introverts as innovators and provided strategies for cultivating creativity and innovation.

In Part IV, we discussed the importance of setting boundaries and practicing mindfulness and self-care to protect your energy and well-being.

In Part V, we explored strategies for creating an introvert-friendly environment and envisioning a more inclusive future for introverts and extroverts.

Throughout this book, we've emphasized the importance of recognizing and embracing your unique strengths and abilities as an introvert. We hope that the insights and strategies provided in this book have helped you on your journey to thriving on your own terms.

Remember, you have the power to shape your life and create the environment and relationships that support your introverted nature. By setting clear boundaries, practicing self-care, and cultivating meaningful connections, you can live a fulfilling and satisfying life as an introvert.

Thank you for taking the time to explore your introverted journey with us, and we wish you all the best on your continued path of self-discovery and growth.

Appendix: Resources for Introverts

Recommended Books Podcasts and Videos

Online Communities and Support Groups

Networking Opportunities for Introverts

Additional tools and resources to continue the self-improvement journey

Appendix: Resources for Introverts
Recommended Books:
- "Quiet: The Power of Introverts in a World That Can't Stop Talking" by Susan Cain
- "The Introvert Advantage: How to Thrive in an Extrovert World" by Marti Olsen Laney
- "Introvert Power: Why Your Inner Life Is Your Hidden Strength" by Laurie Helgoe
- "The Highly Sensitive Person: How to Thrive When the World Overwhelms You" by Elaine N. Aron
- "The Art of Talking to Yourself: Self-Awareness Meets the Inner Conversation" by Vironika Tugaleva

Podcasts and Videos:
- The Introvert, Dear Podcast
- The Introvert Entrepreneur Podcast
- TED Talk: "The Power of Introverts" by Susan Cain
- TED Talk: "The Secret Powers of Introverts" by Scott Kaufman

Online Communities and Support Groups:
- Introvert, Dear Facebook Group
- The Quiet Revolution Community
- Highly Sensitive Refuge Facebook Group
- The Introverted Moms Facebook Group

Networking Opportunities for Introverts:
- LinkedIn Groups for Introverts in Your Industry
- Meetup Groups for Introverts

- Online Professional Networking Events and Webinars
- Conferences and Workshops with Introvert-Friendly Environments

Additional Tools and Resources to Continue the Self-Improvement Journey:

- Insight Timer App for Meditation and Mindfulness Practices
- Moodfit App for Tracking Your Emotional Health and Setting Goals
- 16Personalities Online Personality Test for Understanding Your Unique Traits and Strengths
- Gratitude Journaling Prompts and Exercises for Practicing Gratitude
- Cognitive Behavioural Therapy (CBT) Workbooks and Exercises for Managing Anxiety and Depression

We hope these resources provide you with valuable tools and inspiration to continue your journey towards embracing your introverted nature and thriving on your own terms. Remember to prioritize self-care, set clear boundaries, and celebrate your unique strengths and abilities as an introvert.

Printed in Great Britain
by Amazon